Legislating Love

LEGISLATING *Love*

The Everett Klippert Story

A PLAY
by Natalie Meisner with

DIRECTOR'S NOTES
by Jason Mehmel and

ESSAYS
by Kevin Allen and
Tereasa Maillie

UNIVERSITY OF CALGARY
Press

University of Calgary Press
2500 University Drive NW
Calgary, Alberta
Canada T2N 1N4
press.ucalgary.ca

Library and Archives Canada Cataloguing in Publication

Title: Legislating love : the Everett Klippert story / a play by Natalie Meisner ; with director's notes by Jason Mehmel and essays by Kevin Allen and Tereasa Maillie.
Names: Meisner, Natalie D., 1972– author. | Mehmel, Jason, writer of added commentary. | Allen, Kevin, 1970– writer of added commentary. | Maillie, Tereasa, writer of added commentary.
Series: Brave & brilliant series ; no. 13. ISSN (print) 2371-7238. ISSN (ebook) 2371-7246
Description: Series statement: Brave & brilliant series, ISSN (print) 2371-7238, ISSN (ebook) 2371-7246; no. 13 | Includes bibliographical references.
Identifiers: Canadiana (print) 20190186801 | Canadiana (ebook) 2019019281X | ISBN 9781773850818 (softcover) | ISBN 9781773850825 (PDF) | ISBN 9781773850832 (EPUB) | ISBN 9781773850849 (Kindle)
Classification: LCC PS8576.E433 L44 2019 | DDC C812/.54—dc23

The University of Calgary Press acknowledges the support of the Government of Alberta through the Alberta Media Fund for our publications. We acknowledge the financial support of the Government of Canada. We acknowledge the financial support of the Canada Council for the Arts for our publishing program.

This project was funded by the Government of Alberta through the Alberta Historical Resources Foundation.

Printed and bound in Canada by Marquis
♻ This book is printed on Lynx Opaque Ultra Smooth Cream paper

Editing by Kathryn Simpson
Page design, typesetting, and back cover design by Garet Markvoort, zijn digital
Front cover design by Melina Cusano
Cover art by Scott Sharp

Contents

Legislating Love:
The Everett Klippert Story

A Play by Natalie Meisner

He was born 50 years too soon.
What a disservice to a beautiful human being.

—Katherine Griebel, Everett Klippert's niece,
from "Everett Klippert's Story," by John Ibbitson,
Globe and Mail, 27 February 2016

Character Background

Everett George Klippert, the last man imprisoned in Canada for being gay, and William Wuttunee, who served as his legal counsel, are real people. In basing characters on these real people, all efforts have been made to work with and respect what we know to be historically true. Below, you will find an introduction to these two people and their historical context. Like any portrayal of historical characters, *Legislating Love* offers one possible depiction of many. The other characters (Tonya, Maxine, Handsome, Constable) are invented but plausible characters that emerged out of the meeting between research and imagination.

Everett George Klippert (6 September 1926–7 August 1996)

Everett George Klippert was the last person in Canada to be arrested, charged, prosecuted, convicted, and imprisoned for gross indecency before Bill C-150 was introduced and decriminalized homosexual acts between men over the age of consent of 21. Public outcry at Klippert's conviction was, in part, responsible for the historic pronouncement by Pierre Elliott Trudeau that there was "no place for the state in the bedrooms of the nation."

Mr. Klippert was a beloved bus driver on his downtown route in Calgary, and took care to point out local attractions and to brighten the days of his passengers. Riders frequently report letting an earlier bus pass them so that they could ride with Klippert. He played on the family baseball team, and was everyone's favourite uncle.

Another distinguishing feature of Klippert, and one that set him apart from his contemporaries, was his honesty. While many people hid their homosexuality to avoid violence, job loss, and family estrangement, when Klippert was questioned by police he told the truth. He was repaid for this honesty with eighteen convictions of "gross indecency"— the term for sexual contact short of intercourse (which was classed as a separate offence, and termed "buggery"). Each conviction carried a four-year sentence. Klippert served these concurrently, and was released after four years.

After his release Klippert left Calgary for a fresh start in the Canadian North, but his past dogged him. When questioned by RCMP about a fire in the neighbourhood he ending up admitting to having sex with men and was once again charged and jailed. Though Klippert was in no way inclined to violence, he did admit to being solely attracted to men—and for this admission alone Justice John Sissons reasoned that if released Klippert would likely seek out male partners, and had him designated as a "dangerous sexual offender." This designation carried a life sentence, and Klippert was the only person to be so classified simply for homosexual acts.

The Canadian public was aware that both the UK and the US had decriminalized homosexuality, and Klippert's designation and sentence seemed like step backward for civil rights in Canada. There was a public outcry that "Gentle Klippert," as the papers called him, could be given a life sentence. His case and the public outrage that it sparked led to the decriminalization of homosexuality in Canada in 1969. By the time he was finally released, laws were changing—and so was public opinion. It was the heyday of gay liberation. Everett, however, wanted nothing to do with public life. He declined to be interviewed and rebuffed all attempts to have his place in history recognized publicly.

William Wuttunee (8 May 1928–31 October 2015)

William Wuttunee was born on Red Pheasant First Nation, located in the Treaty 6 territories of Saskatchewan, but forced to leave his family to attend residential school. In 1948 he was awarded a scholarship to attend McGill University, and he made his way to Montreal by freight train. He was one of only two Indigenous students attending university in Canada at the time. After completing his studies in Montreal, he returned west to attend the University of Saskatchewan, where he obtained his degree in law in 1952. Called to the bar in 1954, he became the first Indigenous lawyer in Canada, and was also the first Indigenous lawyer to appear before the Supreme Court of Canada.

Wuttunee practiced law until the 1980s. In addition to his distinguished legal career, he is also known for his controversial book *Ruffled Feathers: Indians in Canadian Society* (Calgary: Bell Books, 1971), for sitting on the Oversight Committees for the Truth and Reconciliation Commission, and for his lifelong dedication to improving the lives of Indigenous peoples across Canada.

The Setup

Maxine, an aspiring historian, is working on Canadian LGBTQ2 history when she discovers Everett George Klippert's story and begins researching his legal case. Via first-person interviews with his family and people he knew, Maxine attempts to find out who Klippert was beyond the court documents and newspaper headlines. Meanwhile, she meets and falls in love with Tonya, a comedian of Métis heritage. She encounters one particularly compelling person, Handsome—an ex-lover of Klippert—who illuminates history for her.

Characters

EVERETT KLIPPERT: A man of average height/build with dark hair. He went by his first name, Everett, for most of his life but after being released from prison went by George.

HANDSOME: Klippert's contemporary and lover.

MAXINE: An aspiring professor of Canadian history.

TONYA: A comedian of Métis ancestry.

CONSTABLE: A Calgary Police officer.

ARMSTRONG: A Police officer from Pine Point, Northwest Territories.

WILLIAM WUTTUNEE: The first Indigenous lawyer in Canada and also one of the only lawyers willing to take Mr. Klippert's case.

Note: the play can be staged with four actors with the use of cross casting such as:

MAXINE/CONSTABLE
HANDSOME/ARMSTRONG
WUTTUNEE/TONYA

Setting

The play exists in several timelines:

1: Handsome, Maxine, and Tonya live in present-day Calgary.
2: Everett Klippert's life at various stages in Calgary and Pine Point (NWT) in the early and mid-1960s.
3: Everett Klippert speaks to the audience from a timeless/ever-present space.

Note on the staging: Everett never leaves the stage, though when he is not involved the lights fade on him as he sits on his bunk. He is sometimes reading the newspaper, sometimes rolling himself a cigarette, sketching, or dozing. He is in another stage-place and time, but as the play progresses we sometimes wonder if he can (almost) see and hear what's happening, and he may subtly react to what is happening.

Scene 1
(*just 'cause something is a rule*)

We hear the hissing air breaks of a city bus coming to a stop. EVERETT *wears a bus driver's hat and coat from the early sixties.*

EVERETT: Can I let you in on a secret? I love my job. I love being the man who drives the bus, the guy who gets everyone where they need to be on time and with a smile on their face. The Calgary Transit Code of Conduct states: "Drivers are to maintain a sunny disposition toward passengers" but I'd do it even if I didn't have to. I take it as a personal challenge to brighten the day of every single rider who steps onto my bus.

[*Pause.*]

In fact you can look at life like one big bus ride. It's what happens between point A and point B … that's up to us.

[*He speaks as if into a bus* PA *system to passengers.*]

Good afternoon, beautiful ladies and fine gents! This is Everett Klippert, your friendly Calgary Transit System operator. We are cruising through our bee-you-ti-ful shiny city at the foot of the Rocky Mountains on Route Number One. Our state of the art new diesel powered coach will take you in luxury and comfort along the scenic Bow River and through the heart of our downtown. Let me know if there is anything I can do to make your ride with us today more pleasant.

[*He puts down the* PA.]

I look in the rearview mirror and see a young man running to make the stop. It's cold and he looks kind of beaten down and discouraged. He sees he won't make it. Gives up and starts walking. His shoulders seem weary, as if he's tired of keeping all that he feels and all that he wants to say locked deep in the strongbox of his own heart.

Or is that me?

Now the rule book says: a city transit driver may not delay the schedule of the bus to accommodate a single passenger. I should pull away …

But life has enough hard edges, don't you think?

[*Hissing air breaks as* EVERETT *stops the bus and opens an imaginary bus door. A handsome man gets on in his work clothes, shivering in the prairie cold.*]

HANDSOME: [*climbing on board*] Brrr! It's a cold one out there. Thanks for waiting.

EVERETT: Climb on board and warm yourself. Now tell me, what is the difference between a bus driver and a cold?

HANDSOME: I'm sure I don't know, friend.

EVERETT: One knows the stops … the other stops the nose.

[*It is a cheesy joke, but* HANDSOME *appreciates it, is cheered by it. He fishes for bus fare.*]

HANDSOME: I hate to have to be the one to tell you this, but you better not quit your day job.

EVERETT: No intention whatsoever.

[HANDSOME *sits and then:*]

HANDSOME: Say a fellow wanted to have a drink in peace. [*He looks around and lowers his voice*] With other men. Do you know where he might go?

EVERETT: If I were that fellow [*looking in the rearview*] I would take myself off to the bar of the Hotel Palliser. I can let you off half a block from there.

HANDSOME: That would be swell. Might be that I see you there sometime then?

EVERETT: You never know. Maybe one of these days.

HANDSOME: And thanks again for waiting for me, I was about froze.

EVERETT: Don't mention it.

HANDSOME: I know it's not allowed, as a rule.

EVERETT: Just because something is a rule, that don't always make it right.

[*Lights fade.*]

Scene 2
(*my left ball*)

Lights come up on MAXINE, *an aspiring professor holding a clipboard, and* HANDSOME, *a well-dressed older gentleman. They sit in a sunny, well-appointed room in an upscale senior citizen's complex. There are pictures and certificates on the wall.*

MAXINE: Thank you so much for agreeing to this meeting.

[*HANDSOME waves as if to say "don't worry about it."*]

HANDSOME: I've knocked a gaping hole in my busy social calendar just for you.

MAXINE: It's very exciting to find a contemporary of Mr. Klippert's and a member of the LGBTQ2 community.

HANDSOME: Now there's a mouthful.

MAXINE: Yes the terms are always evolving, aren't they?

HANDSOME: Evolving. [*a snort or other sounds of understatement*] That's one way to put it.

[*MAXINE makes a note.*]

MAXINE: Okay, great. This brings us to one of the things the study is trying to capture, actually: how do you identify, exactly.

HANDSOME: How do I identify what?

MAXINE: Yourself. Do you prefer to be addressed as gay?

HANDSOME: Ah, I see where you're going …

MAXINE: Some prefer queer or gender fluid—

HANDSOME: [*considering*] I really just prefer cocksucker.

[*A pause. MAXINE looks up from her notepad.*]

MAXINE: Are you being serious or …

HANDSOME: Or?

[*There is a pause. MAXINE hopes for Handsome to fill it but HANDSOME enjoys not doing so. Seeing no other way forward she tries for a reset.*]

MAXINE: I am really happy you agreed to meet. It gets harder and harder to find gay people who lived through the 60s.

HANDSOME: [*nodding*] Very inconvenient for you. How we keep dying.

MAXINE: I'm sorry, that didn't land how I imagined—

HANDSOME: Fact of life, people die. Go on.

MAXINE: I feel fortunate to have found contemporaries of Mr. Klippert, anyone at all who lived through the 60s to go on record.

HANDSOME: Oh, I haven't decided.

MAXINE: —a human subject is an exciting prospect for someone who spends her days wading through clippings and microfiche—What?

HANDSOME: To go on record … I haven't decided yet.

MAXINE: But the release form that I sent—

HANDSOME: You send twelve pages of 10 point font to a senior citizen? [*examines his hands*] What do you expect?

MAXINE: But you agreed to meet with me Mr. —

[*HANDSOME holds up his hands.*}

HANDSOME: You can call me Handsome. Someone should.

MAXINE: Ok Mr. … Handsome.

[*MAXINE is quiet for a moment, trying to get her footing in the conversation.*]

HANDSOME: You never imagine it will happen to you, then it does.

MAXINE: What's that?

HANDSOME: Getting old. A word of warning, time is precious: don't waste a moment.

MAXINE: Of?

HANDSOME: Youth! Health! Life! I mean what are you doing sitting here talking to me, get the hell out of here and go get laid right now. Go on!

MAXINE: You want me to leave, sir?

HANDSOME: Don't call me that. Unless you want to shine my shoes or something, in which case …

MAXINE: You do know why I'm here …

HANDSOME: Yes your school project—Think we might need to keep this for the joke to play?

MAXINE: University study, actually. A qualitative look at sexuality on the prairies—

HANDSOME: Fan-cy.

MAXINE: And if you don't mind I'd like to record our sessions on my phone—

HANDSOME: No. No recordings.

MAXINE: Alright, I understand. I can use a notepad. You are interested in being interviewed, though, right?

HANDSOME: Oh, the staff come in. Very attractive orderly comes in this morning and asks after my children. They're doing fine. Asks after my dear wife … well she's passed away many years ago which I've told him already but no matter. Poor fellow remains entirely tone deaf to my varied attempts at innuendo. I hate to see you go but I love to watch you leave I say and … nothing. Or he gets it and he's pretending not to. I suppose they train them to be neutral. But I am ready to put my eyes out … from sheer boredom.

MAXINE: So you've agreed to talk to me … because you're bored.

HANDSOME: Why not?

MAXINE: But you won't be part of the study.

HANDSOME: I may. I haven't decided yet. First I have a question for you. I'll live slightly longer if I let them take it. But what would be the point of living at all …

MAXINE: I beg your pardon?

HANDSOME: They already got one and now they are coming for the other one … I knew it was only a matter of time.

MAXINE: [looks around] I'm sorry …

HANDSOME: I get phone calls. My daughter, the grandchildren start up now too. It has to go, they say. Quality of life, so on and so forth. But I went to one session of a support group for people who had lost both. And let me tell you there was not a smile in that whole group. It's still mine, after all. I should have the right to keep it, right?

MAXINE: I'm sorry, you've lost me. Keep what?

HANDSOME: My left ball, sweetheart. What else does a man have a set of that he treasures above all else?

MAXINE: I see. [looks around] You want me to weigh in. On whether or not you get to keep your testicle?

HANDSOME: If you please.

MAXINE: At which point you may or may not agree to be a participant in my study.

HANDSOME: That's right. Take a chance. Life is full of uncertainties.

MAXINE: I'm sorry. They didn't tell me you were ill. You must have …

HANDSOME: Cancer, yes. Prostate cancer. No one wants to say it out loud. As if the word alone could summon Beelzebub to your door. Anyway, answer the question.

MAXINE: Although it seems prudent to consider the advice of your doctors … I do believe you have the right—every individual has the right to make decisions about their body.

[*Pause. HANDSOME is thinking about something.*]

HANDSOME: An opinion at last. I was about to toss you out. Now I have two other … we can call them requests if you like, but to be frank, they're demands.

MAXINE: Alright, I'm game: Let's hear them.

HANDSOME: Number one and this is the most important one and you've already come dangerously close to violating it. No whining.

MAXINE: But I'm not whining, Mr. … Handsome.

[*HANDSOME holds up hand.*]

HANDSOME: Ah Ah. Hear that tone? Chest voice, throat voice if you must—but never the nose, darling. Never the nose. This place. Art on the walls, good art even. We pay for it, after all. But they are over-zealous with the decorum. Hard to find someone to cuss with and I miss it so number two: you have to cuss with me.

MAXINE: I'm not sure I can do that—

HANDSOME: You see the door. You are familiar with how it works? Grab the knob firmly and twist.

MAXINE: It would put me in an awkward position.

HANDSOME: We spend our lives in various awkward positions, dear. Be a bit dull otherwise.

MAXINE: Protocol for interviews with human subjects—

HANDSOME: Bye bye school project—

MAXINE: It's not—

HANDSOME: No skin off my nose.

MAXINE: With all due respect.

HANDSOME: Have you ever noticed that what a person says "with all due respect" they are about to say something completely lacking in human decency.

[*MAXINE shakes her head, tries to interject;* HANDSOME *stops her.*]

And when someone says "no offence, but" you better brace yourself for the dirty bitch slap.

[*MAXINE is smiling.*]

Well?

MAXINE: You're—

HANDSOME: A prick? That's the consensus on the floor here among my new ... what do I call them? Neighbours? Not quite. Fellow inmates? But I interrupted you, go on.

MAXINE: This conversation hasn't gone anything like I expected.

HANDSOME: I have surprised you.

MAXINE: Yes.

[*Pause.*]

HANDSOME: Well that's something. Would I prefer a strapping shirt-less hunk sitting in your place and hanging on my every salacious word? I would, honestly, but times being desperate as they are then an earnest baby dyke with a clipboard will do ... Now. Just say it with me one time.

MAXINE: Say what?

HANDSOME: Cocksucker.

MAXINE: Sir ...

HANDSOME: Just say it! What are you, afraid?

MAXINE: Of course not.

HANDSOME: They won't throw you out. This is my room: my once vast, now shrinking domain …

MAXINE: I am not going to say that.

HANDSOME: Oh come on, words aren't dirty unless you make them that way. Both words are beautiful. Cock. Sucker. Put them together it's like whipped cream on fresh strawberries. You worried someone will hear you?

MAXINE: Of course not.

HANDSOME: Because that will kill you faster than cancer.

MAXINE: I am not worried about what people think.

HANDSOME: Oh aren't you? What do people call me? Where shall I pee? What pronoun shall I use? Where are your big-knuckled stone butches? Your glorious broad-shouldered drag queens smashing the cherries off the cop cars? No, no now that all the hard stuff is done, you all scuttle off to the suburbs to get married and have rug rats and forget all about what came before.

MAXINE: That's not fair—

HANDSOME: Chest voice, chest voice—see there it is again. Imagine if we'd said "That's not fair" to the good old boys in the pick-up trucks when they jumped out of their cars during stampede howling for blood?

[*Pause; MAXINE is silent.*]

That's the problem with your generation. You're paralyzed with fear about how people see you.

MAXINE: My generation, the whole thing.

HANDSOME: By and large.

MAXINE: Not that we're hurling out huge inflammatory generalizations or anything.

HANDSOME: [*beat*] No, we wouldn't want that. Scotch? My own stash, you can't get anything decent in the cafeteria. Sorry, the café if you please.

[*MAXINE hesitates for a moment, but then:*]

MAXINE: Sure.

HANDSOME: [*getting glasses*] If we'd stood around fighting with one another when the cops raided the bathhouses? If we fought with each other about how to arrange the letters in the GLGBTT alphabet soup when the boys with the baseball bats rolled up, what do you suppose?

[*MAXINE is silent. HANDSOME pours.*]

They would have split our skulls open on the street like a couple warm eggs in a hot pan, my dear.

[*During this passage, we see EVERETT alone in his cell. He gets up, goes to the mirror, and goes through the motions of shaving. Now as at certain other times during the play when he is being directly discussed, we have the idea that he hears what transpires ... in a way. Or maybe he is thinking about something related.*]

MAXINE: [*she draws in her breath, takes this in*] I can ... imagine.

HANDSOME: Ice?

[*MAXINE waves him off. HANDSOME approves.*]

MAXINE: No thank you. Now I know that Mr. Klippert himself avoided the spotlight.

HANDSOME: He wouldn't like all this fuss, no.

[*EVERETT, shaving, shakes his head at himself in the mirror.*]

MAXINE: But though he never intended it, his case was instrumental in the decision to decriminalize homosexuality.

HANDSOME: Everett was a man, not a case.

[*EVERETT gives himself a post-shave pat on the cheek—as if to tell himself "buck up." His movements are beautiful, in an everyday way.*]

Understated, they give us a sense of how a thinking person makes his way thought all the minutes and hours in a day while incarcerated.]

MAXINE: I really didn't mean—[*she breaks off, puts her hand on her forehead for a moment*] My interview skills aren't ... I should have been more clear with the consent forms. I'm sorry ...

[*MAXINE is starting to pack up. HANDSOME reaches forward and stays her hand. They look into one another's eyes.*]

HANDSOME: Calm down, I was just taking the piss. [*beat*] I'm warming up to you, actually.

MAXINE: You are? [*beat*] What would it be like if you didn't. [*opens notebook*] You must have heard about the apology from the prime minister's office.

HANDSOME: Yes I did. [*pause*] I went and cashed my sorry cheque at the bank, too, and bought a lot of sorry nothing.

MAXINE: No apology makes up for the injustices of the past. But a full pardon makes a difference doesn't it? For those convicted of "gross indecency" before the law changed?

HANDSOME: A great fat lot of good an apology will do Everett.

MAXINE: But it helps his family who fought for his release? Maybe it helps the rest of us, too.

[*Pause, HANDSOME considers this and then:*]

HANDSOME: What is it you want to know?

MAXINE: Were you and Mr. Klippert intimately involved?

[*HANDSOME raises an eyebrow.*]

[*EVERETT, on his bunk, now lays down and closes his eyes.*]

HANDSOME: Perhaps. Do you want to know about that? Do you want to know what we did, what he liked? You dirty little beast.

MAXINE: I am more looking for context—

HANDSOME: Oh drat—

MAXINE: You see I have scoured the court documents and there is a firm historical record that can be constructed via news articles. But how he lived, what he thought, what the texture of his days would have been like … In short, I'm hoping you can help me get to know the real Everett Klippert.

HANDSOME: The real thing, eh? You are nothing if you're not earnest. [*he sips*] We have a couple choices. I can tell you a version that you can print, but that will bore you to tears.

MAXINE: I don't want that.

HANDSOME: Or all the juicy details you won't be able to print—

MAXINE: But—

HANDSOME: Or we can just let it rip, see what happens.

MAXINE: Let's do that.

HANDSOME: But at the end, I get the director's cut.

MAXINE: Meaning?

HANDSOME: When you are finished, you have to give it to me and I cross out anything I need to.

[*MAXINE considers and then:*]

MAXINE: Okay.

[*HANDSOME clinks Maxine's glass as the lights fade.*]

Scene 3
(*a world of handshakes*)

EVERETT sits on his bunk in prison. He is sketching. A piece of charcoal and a partially finished sketchpad on his small table.

EVERETT: Ever since I can remember I have felt this way. And ever since I can remember I have been told that what I feel … is wrong in the eyes of other men. A sin and a crime and a shame for my family. The law says so, the good book too. Doctors and lawyers and policemen. Good men whose job it is to protect us all agree: a homosexual is the worst thing you can be.

[*A sliver of light is coming through his window and hitting the floor. He is trying to capture perspective and uses his thumb and finger to measure something on the sketch.*]

But to me it feels natural. I never wanted to cause a fight or make trouble. If you could close your eyes and imagine … whoever it is that you have that special feeling for … from your nose to your toes … imagine that you're never allowed to touch them again. [*beat*] Not without taking on the whole world in a bareknuckle fistfight before breakfast. [*beat*] Not without losing your home, your family, your friends, your job, your dignity, and your freedom.

Could you go against what your heart and your body are telling you? Maybe you've tried it. Maybe you've had to. Could you live without ever touching another human being again? Live in a world of handshakes or claps on the back? Maybe you could but it's a cold world. A lonely one. Especially for someone with a warm heart.

[*EVERETT picks up his sketch pad and resumes his work as the lights crossfade to:*]

Scene 4
(*the good parts*)

A takeout restaurant piled to the roof with yellow boxes. Above the counter a neon sign announces: CHICKEN ON THE WAY. *Nearby is a giant ceramic statue of a chicken with its chest thrust forward.*

MAXINE *and* TONYA *wait in line for their food. Maxine is checking Tonya out, but trying not to get caught. Finally she speaks.*

MAXINE: So do you uh … come here often?

TONYA: [*looking up from her phone*] What's that?

MAXINE: I just asked if you come here often, which sounds uh … I mean what do you like? What's good here.

TONYA: The place is called "Chicken on the Way." You come for the steak tartar?

[*MAXINE freezes up. TONYA waits for a split second, then turns back to her phone.*]

MAXINE: Oh, steak tartar!

[*TONYA acknowledges her in a conversation-ending way, still on her phone.*]

No that was really funny. You could be a comedian.

TONYA: I am.

[*Beat.*]

MAXINE: Oh, okay. That's … cool. You mean that's your job, or …

TONYA: Or what? Passion? Calling? Feel better if I say hobby? [*beat*] On the other hand I could be pulling your leg, right now.

MAXINE: Actually … I have been standing here trying to find the nerve to strike up a conversation with you but I uh … chickened out.

[*This lands with a thud; TONYA looks up, examines Maxine.*]

[*MAXINE nudging: "I made a joke"*] Chickened out, get it?

TONYA: I did, sadly. You better not give up your day job. If, in fact, you have one.

MAXINE: I do, I teach at the uni.

TONYA: Oh yeah, whatcha teach?

MAXINE: History. Canadian history, which everyone says sounds a bit like an oxymoron, but—

TONYA: How's that?

MAXINE: Just that our history, in comparison to the long and storied pasts of other nations, is relatively short.

TONYA: Drank the Settler Kool Aid, did ya?

MAXINE: No, don't get me wrong—

TONYA: Plenty of people here on Turtle Island telling stories long before the settlers got here with the poxy blankets.

MAXINE: I didn't know you were, I mean …

TONYA: Go on.

[*MAXINE shakes her head. She knows she is wading in deeper.*]

You were about to make a staggering assumption about my identity based on … what? My hair colour?

MAXINE: No.

TONYA: Skin tone? Blood quantum?

MAXINE: No, please! Just a silly joke at the expense of historians, but I can see how totally reprehensible—from a First Nations perspective. No, Indigenous is the preferred term now, right?

[*A pause. TONYA lets Maxine hang.*]

TONYA: You asking me? Or telling me?

MAXINE: Asking! Of course.

TONYA: Refreshing. [*beat*] But I think I'll let you do your own homework.

MAXINE: Fair. [*beat*] Look, I have an involuntary tic, or let's call it a dubious gift, for saying the wrong thing. But I do *know* we've only begun to scratch the surface of the injustices of the past and I'm sorry.

TONYA: You people love yourself some apologies. Sorry, sorry always sorry. What are you sorry for?

MAXINE: All of it.

TONYA: That's a lot to answer for. Plus sorry doesn't mean much unless you take action.

MAXINE: I know, reparation is complicated. Might not ever be fully possible, but we …

[*TONYA is silent.*]

Can you please say … something. Anything.

TONYA: It's kind of fun to watch … the more you struggle the deeper you sink.

MAXINE: Oh, fuuuuck …

TONYA: Like a dinosaur. In a tar pit.

MAXINE: If I, as one individual, look you in the eye and say I am sorry? Doesn't that count for something?

TONYA: [*considering*] It does.

MAXINE: And I don't agree with what's happened.

TONYA: Is happening.

MAXINE: [*corrects herself*] Is happening. To your people? Who are your people, by the way.

TONYA: I'm Métis. Come on, I'll tell you about it on the way.

MAXINE: [*appreciating*] "On the way" … I see what you did there—

TONYA: You have to work it into the batter, not nail it on the nose. So, tell me professor—

MAXINE: Oh no, please, I am a lowly contract worker grinding it out at the poverty line on sessional appointments … with a slim chance of gaining a permanent employment.

TONYA: Why is that?

MAXINE: Education system being dismantled under our feet … creeping co-option of intellectual life. Plus my work isn't … popular.

TONYA: What's popular got to do with teaching at the uni?

MAXINE: You're familiar with the phrase "history is written by the winners"?

TONYA: Sounds familiar, yeah.

MAXINE: The people I find compelling are often … I seem to keep falling for the losers.

TONYA: Wow, is that … what passes for a pick-up line in your world?

MAXINE: Wait, I wasn't. I mean I'm not—

TONYA: No? Okay, my mistake. [*goes back to her phone*]

[*A beat.*]

[*MAXINE tries again.*]

MAXINE: I mean I *was* trying to talk to you but I wasn't trying to pick you up. Which isn't to say that I don't find you … Why do I do this. Every time I meet a beautiful woman? [*beat*] Am I speaking out loud? I am. I have totally messed this up, haven't I?

TONYA: Maybe. Come here.

[*TONYA crooks her finger, MAXINE leans toward her.*]

So what are you into? The dark meat? The light? Little of both?

MAXINE: Whaaat … ?

[*TONYA turns to face Maxine, suddenly in full-on flirt mode.*]

TONYA: You asked me what's good here. Some like the thigh … you can really get your teeth into that. But my personal favourite is the breast.

[*TONYA snaps her teeth together.*]

MAXINE: Oh my god.

[*TONYA leans forward, takes Maxine's hand.*]

TONYA: You poor thing. I have been checking you out all the way through the lineup. Let's get out of here.

MAXINE: Uh—

TONYA: Here's the part where you say yes.

MAXINE: But I just uttered some of the most unenlightened things a person could ever—

TONYA: [*holds up her hand*] Just yes.

MAXINE: Yes. [*beat*] Oh, now? You mean like now.

TONYA: Don't you sometimes just wish you could skip all the bullshit? Skip right to the good parts?

MAXINE: That sounds … wow, great … but to be sure we're on the same page here, can you define good parts?

TONYA: Well we would usually stop this conversation right now, exchange digits and begin the weird mating dance of the modern lesbian. Coffee first, right? Or tea. No full meals, no booze. Only light chit chat. Then we both run home creep one another's social media for obvious signs of wack-O. None noted, we move on to dinner, but only after a waiting period because god forbid one of us two dykes seems interested or, lord above, *eager*. All this usually takes four to six weeks. [*beat*] After which, we just throw in the towel and move in together.

MAXINE: Move in?

TONYA: We both know the U-Haul hangs over the first moment of any lesbian flirtation. [*points*] See, there it is. A great big orange and white piano in the sky waiting to fall on our heads. So we find a place, go splits on a sofa. We get a mutual cat. A co-cat, if you will. Name him George.

MAXINE: Stop! This is madness!

TONYA: What?

MAXINE: George is a terrible name for a cat.

TONYA: But we don't have to be those lesbians.

MAXINE: We don't?

[*TONYA shakes her head as two boxes skim across the counter. She takes out her wallet and tosses a bill. They go outside.*]

TONYA: Do you believe we were meant to meet here today?

MAXINE: I don't, personally, find belief a reliable instrument with which to navigate the world … [*she looks at Tonya, tries to read her, can't*] I can't tell if you're kidding, or …

TONYA: Ya, that'll probably keep happening. So what if the creator placed us right here, right now … with boxes of chicken in our hands as some kind of test?

MAXINE: I honour and respect all your ways of knowing, but I should let you know I am a materialist—

TONYA: Sounds serious.

MAXINE: A Marxist-feminist-materialist, in fact, with a strong existential leaning …

TONYA: [*pause, she considers*] But you're pretty cute; we'll get it looked at.

MAXINE: Are we actually having this conversation at Chicken on the Way?

TONYA: Don't knock C.O.T. Dubs. This is a very important place for my people.

MAXINE: You mean this place is built on a sacred site?

TONYA: Built on? Mary Sue, this *is* a sacred site! My grandmother brought me here for a three-piece dinner every Sunday afternoon for my whole childhood. Corn fritters, amen.

MAXINE: Should we … be joking about this??

TONYA: Whatcha wanna hear? Five hundred generations of people hunted, trapped, harvested, lived, and loved here before your people came and stole the land?

MAXINE: Well that's true.

TONYA: Yes, but I can see all the way to end of that conversation. It gets me some earnest commiseration, a shoulder to cry on. What it *doesn't* get me … is hot sex and you making me an omelette in the morning.

MAXINE: In this case … it might, actually.

[*TONYA reaches out her hand and MAXINE takes it, in wonder; they exit together.*]

Scene 5
(*prison limericks*)

EVERETT, on his bunk. He has a notepad and a pencil and writes a letter.

EVERETT: Dear Sis,

Thanks again for filing those appeals. Lord knows where you get the stamina when all they do is slam the door in your face.

Say, if life's a box of chocolates, how come I keep getting the one with the cow patty centre?

[*Pause, he thinks, writes some more.*]

You asked how I am getting along. They let me watch the television now, so I get to see something of the world which is a great relief. The fellows out in the yard get a bang out of picking on a guy like me, but they seem to calm down again if I pay them no mind.

They say if life hands you lemons … You figure there's enough sugar in this world to make lemonade out of this one? Well, now, let's try. The bright side of prison … the bright side of prison. Three square meals a day, though the fare is nothing to write home about. Lots of time to read and write letters to my favourite sister.

Lots of time to write anything I want. Maybe I'll turn my hand to poetry like Aunt Cora?

There once was a young man from Kindersly
Who went about love quite timorously
He fell for a Bloke,
The Trial was a joke
And in jail does he languish perpetually …

[*We hear sounds of prison around him, he grows serious.*]

That wasn't … I'm sorry, sis. I know that's not funny at all when you're working so hard to get me out.

You ask if I have any regrets. Well. I can honestly tell you, I never hurt anyone and I am not sorry for trying to understand what it is that … I am. But I am most truthfully and awfully sorry for the trouble I brought to your door.

[*Lights fade.*]

Scene 6
(*all in the chest*)

HANDSOME'*s room.* MAXINE *looks at a wall of awards and photos of Handsome as a younger man in a construction hat.*

During most of the scene, EVERETT *sits on his bunk on the other half of the stage reading in dim lighting. For most of the scene we don't focus on him, but he may turn a page now and then or change position at moments that underscore Handsome's words.*

MAXINE: [*points out the window*] So your firm did this building? [*HANDSOME nods yes*] And this one.

HANDSOME: That one too.

MAXINE: Quite a legacy.

HANDSOME: [*gestures to a wall of kid and grandkid photos*] There's a legacy for you.

MAXINE: Of course. Beautiful family you have.

HANDSOME: Yeah, they're an okay bunch.

MAXINE: [*looking out the window at the city*] Still this is amazing. You only have to look down over the skyline from here to see your work.

HANDSOME: I look at it [*gestures to skyline*] I see materials lists, man hours. Things we should have done differently. *Stress.*

MAXINE: A tough industry to be in for … for you, I would think.

HANDSOME: Im-fucking-possible.

MAXINE: So you never felt safe in your working life to be open about your sexuality?

HANDSOME: Anywhere. You can't fight everyone. You have to play the hand play dealt. In the trades, they will just cut you out of the food chain. You say to yourself, after I land this one big contract …

MAXINE: Then what?

HANDSOME: The next big one. If I get to the top, make myself indispensable then one fine day I'll be able to say: There, see? I've filled out your pay slips. I've given you your Christmas bonuses. Kicked your ass when you needed it. I took care of you, damn it. See now, a filthy faggot has walked among you all this time … and the sky did not fall.

MAXINE: [*she nods*] And now?

HANDSOME: After my wife passed … things have shifted, I can see that. People are more accepting. I told one man. And what do you think happened? Did he stretch out his hand in understanding and brotherly love?

MAXINE: I'll go with no?

HANDSOME: Kicked me back down to the bottom again. [*turns away, looks out the window, suddenly he is filled with rage and life*] Goddamn it I hate my fellow man some days.

MAXINE: Is today one of those days? 'Cause I could come back another time.

HANDSOME: Sit down you pain in the ass, you're not getting away that easily. Wait a minute now, is it my imagination or did you just try to crack a joke?

MAXINE: I have met someone …

HANDSOME: Oh?

MAXINE: She's a comedian so maybe it's rubbing off.

HANDSOME: Something's rubbing off. I thought something was different. Maybe a haircut, a little personal grooming …

MAXINE: Her name is Tonya. She's smart and funny, and just so …

HANDSOME: You're hot for her.

MAXINE: She's just got this amazing ... energy. She makes you think anything is possible.

HANDSOME: If you like I can boil down the accumulated wisdom of seven decades. Maybe save you some pain?

MAXINE: I'd love that.

HANDSOME: You find somebody that gets your dick hard? [*he raises his hand in an "I'm kidding" gesture to fend off her objections*] va-jay-jay, your lady bits: call it what you like. You find that someone, and you also like them as a person? You grab on tight and don't let them go. Better let your heart stop beating than let that flame go out.

[*MAXINE is writing.*]

Well you're writing it down, anyway. Is it helpful?

MAXINE: Maybe not for the study. I've started a separate file for crucial life advice.

[*Pause.*]

HANDSOME: Okay, then. What else do you want to know?

MAXINE: Where could gay people meet here in the city in the fifties and sixties?

HANDSOME: Nowhere was safe, but we didn't let it stop us. We found one another alright. In locker rooms, in alleyways, in parked cars.

MAXINE: How did you know someone else was gay? Was anyone using the hanky code at that time?

HANDSOME: Nah, not 'til the seventies. [*reflects*] I miss the seventies.

MAXINE: How could you know if your advances were welcome? How could you know that he wouldn't—

HANDSOME: Kick my ass? You had to read body language, look for eye contact ...

MAXINE: [*writing*] Sounds exciting.

HANDSOME: It was! The stroll on the leaf-covered banks of the Bow River. We made love in alleys and bathrooms and on top of the bags of cement being mixed up for the Husky Tower. Every place we could find away from the eyes of the bastards who wanted to kill us.

MAXINE: Who were the bastards?

HANDSOME: Anyone, everyone. If you picked a guy up you had to put him to the test to be sure he wasn't an undercover cop. They trained them to entrap us …

MAXINE: How did you test that?

HANDSOME: Make him put his money where his mouth is, make him go first. Something like that is hard to fake. Was it sweeter, perhaps, because of the danger? I ask myself that sometimes …

MAXINE: [*writing*] Wow—

HANDSOME: But you can't write that, obviously.

MAXINE: [*sighs*] What, why not?

HANDSOME: Everyone will hate you. The straights and the gays. You can't win.

MAXINE: This isn't about winning.

HANDSOME: No? What's it about, then?

MAXINE: Keeping our histories alive. So that every young person who feels same-sex desire doesn't have to feel ashamed and worthless and alone. Like they don't deserve to walk the earth.

HANDSOME: [*pause, he surveys her as if for the first time*] That's how you feel.

MAXINE: We're not here to talk about me.

HANDSOME: Do you?

MAXINE: Sometimes.

HANDSOME: [*shakes he head, reflects*] Even now when you have every-thing at your fingertips.

MAXINE: We don't … never mind. We've talked about your work en-vironment. What about your home life, your wife—

HANDSOME: My wife was a wonderful human being. She gave me my children and my grandchildren and we cared deeply for one another—

[*MAXINE nods, lets his memory of his wife live in the room with them for a moment, and then:*]

MAXINE: She was aware that you had relations with men?

HANDSOME: We didn't speak of it, but we had … an understanding. Sometimes I wonder if she, too …

MAXINE: Might have had feelings for women?

HANDSOME: [*nods*] But whether she ever got to act on them … I wish I could tell you more.

MAXINE: Lavender marriages: a union without intimacy … usually to escape persecution. Nearly every society has them.

HANDSOME: Is that right? Well she never wanted to discuss any of that business. At least it seemed that way to me.

MAXINE: And what about now? Have you thought of opening up to your children? Your grandchildren.

HANDSOME: Nah.

MAXINE: Why not?

HANDSOME: "Guess what, Grampa's gay!" It would be something like a joke.

MAXINE: It's not ever a joke, Handsome. Not then, not now.

HANDSOME: They don't want to be bothered.

MAXINE: Give them a chance? They might surprise you.

[*Pause; HANDSOME considers.*]

What about your own father and mother? Was there anyone you could confide in as a young person?

HANDSOME: My father [*shakes his head, he may laugh or another sound that means "never"*] It's the fathers that mind it most. Mine was a well-known man. A difficult man.

MAXINE: He would have had objections.

HANDSOME: If you call a fist in the mouth an objection.

[*Silence. MAXINE takes this in.*]

In this city, at that time … well every contract depended on your influence. If it got out that his son was a poof, a faggot? Pfft. He'd never let it happen. Now I look out the window on any given day and see you all strolling along the river hand in hand. Right out in the open.

MAXINE: The changes in the law have made life better, to be sure …

HANDSOME: Better? It's a goddamn cakewalk.

[*MAXINE has her head down. She may be tearing up slightly but she does not want to appear unprofessional.*]

MAXINE: Cakewalk, yeah—

HANDSOME: Did I say something to upset you.

MAXINE: No, no I'm fine. Just talking about fathers … My own father and I don't …

HANDSOME: [*quietly pours her another drink*] How long?

MAXINE: Three, no … [*realizing*] four years now.

HANDSOME: He throw you out for being gay?

MAXINE: No, it's not cut and dried like that. He just … well, he'll never say it out loud but he … does not love me.

HANDSOME: You sure about that?

MAXINE: He goes to the rest of the family behind my back, tells them he has objections to my "lifestyle" as he calls it. Well I have objections to his "bigotry" so now … we are in some kind of personal cold war—

[*MAXINE looks down at her notepad. Then pulls herself together.*]

I'm sorry. We're here to look at your past not mine.

HANDSOME: Did you ever think that it might just be … the same task, my dear?

MAXINE: Like you said, we have it easy. No reason to whine.

HANDSOME: That's not whining. What you just told me just now … that was all in the chest.

[*HANDSOME puts his hand on her shoulder. A small yet comforting gesture. MAXINE is quiet and then:*]

Okay. Let's get back on track. I first met Everett in 1961 …

[*EVERETT lowers the newspaper, and looks out to the audience with a subtle smile. It as if he too, in his own time and space is thinking back, with enjoyment to their first meeting.*]

[*EVERETT puts the paper down and steps into the next scene.*]

Scene 7
(*tip of the iceberg*)

Chicken on the Way, looking much the same in the early sixties as it does today. EVERETT stands in line waiting to order. Behind him enters HANDSOME in his work clothes from a construction site. Cold air comes in with him from the street.

EVERETT: The four-piece dinner with extra corn fritters, if you please.

HANDSOME: You going off to eat alone, friend?

[*EVERETT glances around before deciding that the man is, indeed, talking to him.*]

EVERETT: [*recognizes him*] Hey there.

HANDSOME: You're the bus driver, right? "What's the difference between a bus driver and a cold? One knows the stops and the other …

[*They overlap on this next bit—a moment of enjoyment.*]

EVERETT/HANDSOME: … stops the nose."

HANDSOME: That night you stopped for me. I was feeling pretty low.

EVERETT: That a fact?

HANDSOME: Quarrelled with my pa. He threw me out.

EVERETT: I figured something of the kind.

HANDSOME: A kind face … made all the difference.

EVERETT: And how are things now?

HANDSOME: Better! I already got a job, didn't even need the old man's connections.

EVERETT: Well that's grand. Whatcha doing?

HANDSOME: Building the new tower.

EVERETT: You don't say. Tallest in the country when she's done, I hear?

HANDSOME: Never mind that—tallest on the continent.

EVERETT: Man alive!

HANDSOME: Say, I'm a little short for cash. Can you spot a guy a buck.

EVERETT: I can probably do that.

[*EVERETT shakes his head good-naturedly, and hands Handsome a dollar.*]

HANDSOME: That's swell. Pay you back next week, promise. You should see the base of the building. It's like an iceberg.

EVERETT: Iceberg? How's that?

HANDSOME: The bit you see above ground is just a start. More than half of the thing is dug underground. Come on along, we'll sit up in the crane. Drop the chicken bones down into the wet cement.

[*EVERETT looks around to see if others are watching. Looks into Handsome's eyes. Is he for real? Not a cop? Not looking to beat him up?*]

EVERETT: Now there's an idea. Imagine all the little bones preserved deep inside the building, long after we're gone.

HANDSOME: [*leans in*] Nice view and there's no one else around this time of night.

EVERETT: [*to the person making the food offstage*] Make it a twelve piece with slaw and fritters.

[*The men head out into the night with their steaming box of chicken.*]

Scene 8
(*into the beaver*)

A small stage with the standard kit for a stand-up comedian: tall stool, microphone, spotlight. We hear the sounds of a comedy club. People talking, laughing, drinking. TONYA *enters.*

EVERETT, *in his own space, has a paper bag with some popcorn and eats it as if watching. He would, of course, not be watching Tonya ... but he might be watching some other comedian who would have been on the screen on the* TV *in jail. Or is he watching her?*

In the background the sounds of the 60s laugh track are delicately woven together with the sounds of a modern comedy club.

TONYA: [*out to the audience*] Hey there. Hi everyone. If you read the program maybe you might have seen that I'm the only Indigenous person on the ticket tonight. The only dyke, oh, and the only woman too. [*pause*] Hands up if you're worried you're in for a round of man-bashing? Nah, not my deal. Hands up if you're afraid I'll rake you over the coals for your ancestor's crimes? Hands up if you've ever wondered what lesbians do in bed? Hands up if you already know. Hands up if you're just here for the cheap beer?

[TONYA *goes back to the stool, has a sip of water.*]

[EVERETT *sits up on his bunk, leans forward toward the small* TV, *enjoying the show. He may slap his knee.*]

[*And then:*]

People always want to know … are you mad? Kind of a raw deal, right? Broken treaties, forced relocations. But what's a couple of hundred years of colonial exploitation between friends? Let's let bygones be bygones. Times change, march of modernity. [*pause*] And then there's the residential schools—

Okay fuck it, we're mad. There I said it, we're mad.

But that doesn't mean we—you and I, here in this room—can't still be friends, does it? Or does it?

[*Beat.*]

You know my ma didn't have a big reaction when I told her I was a lesbian. "So you're into the beaver instead of the stag, no big deal." But recently I had to break it to her. Not only am I dating a woman … I am dating a white woman. And a professor.

Well that was the last straw. "Oh my God," says ma, "we'll have to be minding our Ps and Qs all the time."

But then she's just like: "Oh well, maybe we can get some help with the Sunday crossword."

And she just grabs her purse and heads out to bingo.

[*Lights fade on* TONYA *as the interwoven sounds of the comedy clubs in two times gently die away.*]

Scene 9
(*bedrooms of the nation*)

MAXINE *and* TONYA *are in bed. It is a sumptuous morning after. Maxine stirs, Tonya is on Maxine's arm. Maxine wakes up, smiles at Tonya gently. She looks at her for a moment, amazed, and then gently tries to extricate herself without waking Tonya. No dice.*

TONYA: Where do you think you're going?

MAXINE: Didn't want to wake you.

TONYA: I didn't think anything could after last night.

MAXINE: You were … wow.

TONYA: No, *you* were wow … come here.

[*MAXINE is still trying for extraction, but* TONYA *is making it diffi-cult. They kiss and are both tempted to call off the morning and just stay in bed, but:*]

MAXINE: While I would love to stay in bed all morning, I have a deadline.

TONYA: Oooh, a deadline.

MAXINE: Have to finish this paper; I've already had two extensions.

TONYA: What's it about?

MAXINE: Policy stuff, kinda boring.

TONYA: Try me.

MAXINE: So in sixty-nine …

TONYA: [*with interest*] Sixty-nine?

MAXINE: *Nineteen* sixty-nine … is the year we think of homosexuality as being decriminalized in Canada.

TONYA: Not even that long ago.

MAXINE: But under Bill C-150: the Criminal Law Amendment Act … Are you sure, it's kind of dry …

[*TONYA touches Maxine under the covers.*]

TONYA: Doesn't feel dry to me …

MAXINE: You're so bad.

TONYA: Admit it: it's a good bad.

MAXINE: Think of the sixties we think of?

TONYA: Peace protests. Woodstock.

MAXINE: The space race, the moon landing.

TONYA: That shit was poorly shot on a Hollywood backlot.

MAXINE: Really? We're going there?

TONYA: Put it past them?

MAXINE: That's a whole different discussion.

TONYA: Fine.

MAXINE: Feminism, The Black Power Movement—

TONYA: The Red Power Movement.

MAXINE: Yes! And often working together. They lived intersectionality before the word was even used. Every liberation discourse we have now was shaking out its wings for flight ...

TONYA: It's so damn hot when you talk like that.

MAXINE: Be serious for a minute.

TONYA: Nineteen sixty-nine was also the year they tried to replace the Indian Act. With ... wait for it ... "The White Paper." How's that for serious?

[*MAXINE grabs a notepad and a pen from her side table, makes a note.*]

MAXINE: Ugh, yes.

TONYA: You can't make that shit up.

MAXINE: Right? Sometimes being a historian is just a process of turning over shovelfuls of shame.

[*During this next section, we see the lights very slowly come up on EVERETT on the other side of the stage. He is on his bunk, in a jail cell. He is reading the newspaper.*

TONYA: Well keep putting your back into it, girl.

MAXINE: You've probably heard "There is no place for the state ...

TONYA/EVERETT: ... in the bedrooms of the nation."

[*Pause.*]

TONYA: Daddy Trudeau.

MAXINE: People think he made it up, but he actually borrowed it from a *Globe & Mail* reporter, one Martin O'Malley. The debate raged in the papers, the courts, and the court of public opinion.

[*During this next section, we see the lights very slowly come up on EVERETT on the other side of the stage. He is on his bunk, in a jail cell. He has his bus driver's hat in his hand. It has sat on his mantel so far, but now he picks it up and dusts it off.*]

And centred itself on the plight of one man:

EVERETT/MAXINE: Everett George Klippert.

MAXINE: He wasn't an activist or a public figure. He was just somebody's son, somebody's brother, somebody's uncle, and the city of Calgary's favourite bus driver.

EVERETT: At your service.

MAXINE: He would tell stories, point out the sites. Riders would let a bus go by and delay their trip, just to start their day with Mr. Klippert. When he was questioned by police, Mr. Klippert did something unheard of: he told the truth.

TONYA: To the cops? Oof, see, you can't do that.

[*EVERETT tosses the hat on the dresser. Sits on his bunk.*]

MAXINE: He admitted his attraction to men, even asked psychologists how they would feel if the tables were turned. This very truthfulness was later used as proof that he would seek out male partners if released and for this alone they labelled him "a dangerous sexual offender."

TONYA: That's terrible.

MAXINE: He got an automatic life sentence.

[*EVERETT has dropped his face into his hands. This is perhaps as low as we see him. He holds his own sides and rocks.*]

There was a public outcry with headlines like: "Gentle Klippert, must he really get life?" His case won over hearts and minds …

TONYA: Wow. A big gay hero, from right here on the prairie.

MAXINE: Everyone kind of assumed, that when the law changed they'd let him go, but they didn't.

TONYA: Why not?

MAXINE: The omnibus bill only referred to what happened in private spaces and yet most gay people met in public. So there's this weird paradox: public acceptance of homosexuals seems to increase, but there is a backlash by law enforcement. It was his sister Leah, a legal secretary, just refusing to give up and filing appeal after appeal that finally got him out after ten years.

[*EVERETT holds his own head in his hands for a moment.*]

TONYA/EVERETT: Ten years …

MAXINE: He moved to Edmonton, got a job as a truck driver, and started using his middle name. Eventually he married a woman quite a few years his senior. A marriage of companionship, his relatives say. Over the years journalists, gay organizations, and filmmakers approached him again and again to illuminate his place in history. He refused every single request.

TONYA: After all that he must have wanted …

TONYA/EVERETT: … to be left alone.

[*EVERETT turns his back to us. Sleeps.*]

MAXINE: And he was until recently. A story in the *Globe and Mail* prompted a wave of research about his life and others like him. There has been a full juridical pardon for every Canadian whose life was mutilated by the so-called "gross indecency" laws.

TONYA: That's a really amazing thing to be a part of.

MAXINE: His family have been really helpful, and then there's Handsome—my guy in the senior's residence. But he's … complicated.

TONYA: Handsome?

MAXINE: He was one of Klippert's lovers.

TONYA: Wow, that's amazing.

MAXINE: But doesn't want to give his name so he asked to use that pseudonym.

TONYA: He makes you call him Handsome?

MAXINE: Yeah and also won't let me use anything from his interviews unless he vets it first.

TONYA: Fair ask.

MAXINE: And he also tried to make me say cocksucker out loud.

TONYA: [*enjoying this*] In the old folks' home?

MAXINE: Assisted living facility, but yes.

TONYA: I like him already.

[*MAXINE is stirring, looking toward her desk.*]

MAXINE: You two would probably get along.

TONYA: Take me to meet him one of those days. Okay, I see you itching to get at it, I'll make coffee.

[*TONYA exits. The light fades to softer on MAXINE as she begins to work again. The lights come up slightly on EVERETT, who speaks to the audience.*]

Scene 10
(*hit by the bus*)

EVERETT is on his bunk with his notebook. He writes lines, crosses them out. This is a draft to pass the time.

EVERETT: If Cupid lines you up with his bow
There's something I want you should know:

call it love,
call it lust
just do what you must,
to avoid being hit by the bus!

[*Lights fade.*]

Scene 11
(*more Handsome*)

A dark alley. At first we see only silhouettes and the glowing ends of cigarettes.

HANDSOME: Still in my work clothes, didn't have time to change.

EVERETT: That's all right.

HANDSOME: Do I reek?

EVERETT: Not so's you'd notice. You working long hours?

HANDSOME: Sure enough. Takes some sweat to make an imprint against this big old sky, but enough of that.

[*HANDSOME pulls Everett to him.*]

EVERETT: Hold on—

HANDSOME: What's the matter?

EVERETT: Just thought we might talk for a minute.

HANDSOME: We're talking. [*laughs*] But you can walk and chew bubble gum at the same time, can't you?

EVERETT: [*pulling away*] Sure, but—

HANDSOME: I'm not much of a conversationalist, whattaya want? A cup of tea and a big old chin wag?

EVERETT: Nah, just like to hear about your life, you know?

HANDSOME: What do you want to know.

EVERETT: Like why you're working from sun up to sun down. What do you care about, what are your dreams?

HANDSOME: I want to build towers of my own.

EVERETT: That a fact?

HANDSOME: Yeah, and I'll do it too. With or without my old man's help.

EVERETT: He in the construction business?

HANDSOME: He *is* the business, in this town anyway. Says I'll amount to nothing. But he'll see. I'll be a man worth knowing one day.

EVERETT: You already are, in my books. [*pause*] My own pa is … well he's a good man but he's also a god-fearing man …

[*He breaks off, closes his eyes for a moment and shakes his head.*]

Sometimes I think if I can just talk to him and explain …

HANDSOME: If I tried explaining this to my father, well it would be pretty simple. He'd take me out behind the barn and shoot me. Like he would a sick animal.

EVERETT: But it's not right. I don't feel sick. Do you?

HANDSOME: No. But it's …

EVERETT: What?

HANDSOME: A flaw. An affliction—

EVERETT: No. Don't say that. [*holds him at arm's length, really looks*] You are altogether handsome. There is no flaw in you.

HANDSOME: [*punches him gently on the arm*] Come on now.

EVERETT: Don't you ever wonder why we have to hide away like this? We aren't hurting anyone, after all.

HANDSOME: You are a thinker, alright. I'll give you that. A real deep thinker. [*beat*] I can't see as how it's going to do you much good.

EVERETT: Why? Why has life got to be like this for us homosexuals?

HANDSOME: Don't you call me that.

[*HANDSOME grabs Everett by the mouth and squeezes.*]

Let's get something real clear right now. I'm not one of your kind. Ask anyone, and I was never here tonight. Ask anyone and I am pulling a double shift down at the work site, ankle deep in concrete.

[*Releases him.* EVERETT *rubs his jaw.*]

EVERETT: Alright, then. You don't have to be sore about it.

HANDSOME: Everett, if anyone ever asks you about me—

EVERETT: [*winks*] Never heard of you. Don't worry your secret's safe with me.

HANDSOME: [*more softly*] Why do you talk so damn much? Don't you see it's the naming makes everyone upset. It's the naming that makes it dirty.

EVERETT: Well there's where we'll have to agree to disagree. Because I truly believe that things become more beautiful—

HANDSOME: Aw, come off it.

EVERETT: Handsome, then. Things become more handsome when you name them.

[*Beat.*]

[*Lights fade on them;* HANDSOME *exits.*]

Scene 12
(*stone around your neck*)

Lights fade up on EVERETT *in his cell. He has a stack of books and among them, a bible.*

EVERETT: I was taught to always tell the truth. Especially to the authorities. The firemen, the policemen, out there every day trying to project us. They are just doing their jobs, after all.

"Do not lie, do not cheat, do not deceive one another." Leviticus 19:11

If you tell one lie, you have to remember it word for word. It is a pebble, then a stone, and finally a boulder around your neck. Each time you tell the lie, it gets just that little bit heavier. You have to tell it exactly the same way or the jig is up. Tell another lie and you add another pebble, stone, boulder. Keep lying and you'll have the world's heaviest necklace.

You'll stagger under the weight. Scarcely able to move an inch! But if you stick to the truth you walk the earth a free man: light on your feet without a care in the world.

[*Lights fade.*]

Scene 13
(*Christmas bus*)

A bare table and a couple chairs in a police questioning room.

CONSTABLE: State your full name and occupation.

EVERETT: Everett George Klippert. I am a bus driver for Calgary Transit.

CONSTABLE: And before that?

EVERETT: I worked over at the dairy, officer.

CONSTABLE: Kind of a dirty job. You like to get your hands dirty, Klippert?

EVERETT: Cows are very clean animals, actually. Still I love driving the bus more.

CONSTABLE: You must meet a lot of people.

EVERETT: Yes sir; it's the best job I ever had!

CONSTABLE: A lot of men.

EVERETT: I try to make the day of every passenger—man, woman, or child—just that little bit brighter.

CONSTABLE: How exactly do you do that?

EVERETT: With a greeting or a joke. Shall I tell you one of my old standbys?

CONSTABLE: We don't have time for jokes, Mr. Klippert.

EVERETT: I suppose not, in your line of work.

CONSTABLE: I deal with criminals every day. Give a criminal the idea that the law is a joke … well I guess he figures he can carry on breaking it.

[*EVERETT is quiet.*]

[*CONSTABLE looks at his notepad.*]

If I contacted your employer, he'd give me a good report of you?

EVERETT: I'm not one to toot my own horn. But I have been selected employee of the month. This year I get to drive the Christmas bus.

CONSTABLE: The Christmas bus?

EVERETT: Let you in on a little secret. We don't actually have the real Jolly Old Elf on board.

CONSTABLE: Can you stick to answering the question?

EVERETT: The Christmas bus, sir, drives down Route 1 wrapped in a giant red bow, and the ride is offered at the discount rate of a nickel. Calgary Transit's way of saying Merry Christmas to the people of our great city. A small thing, but it really gets folks in the spirit.

[*Shaking his head.*]

CONSTABLE: Indeed. I'll need a full account of your whereabouts yesterday.

EVERETT: I was at work for most of the day. Listen, has there been an accident? Has someone been hurt?

CONSTABLE: I'll be asking the questions here. Start at sunrise and go from there.

EVERETT: I got up and went straight to work, drove my route until dinnertime. Then I ate at bus barn canteen with the other fellows …

CONSTABLE: And then?

EVERETT: I went out.

CONSTABLE: Out where?

EVERETT: Just walking …

CONSTABLE: That answer is not going to pass muster. You walked where and with who?

EVERETT: With a friend.

CONSTABLE: A man, I take it.

EVERETT: Yes.

CONSTABLE: So what did you and he get up to, then? And does he have a name?

EVERETT: Of course he has a name.

CONSTABLE: I am losing patience, tell me the man's name.

EVERETT: I … can't.

CONSTABLE: Why not?

EVERETT: On account of I promised not to. And on account of I don't want you to go after him too.

CONSTABLE: Mr. Klippert, I am not "going after" anyone. I am an officer in the line of duty following up on a [*glances down*] very serious allegation made by an upstanding man of this community. Now if you haven't done anything wrong … If your "friend" hasn't done anything wrong then there's no need to be concerned. Did he?

EVERETT: Did he what?

CONSTABLE: Do anything wrong?

EVERETT: No, sir.

CONSTABLE: Then tell me his name. Unless you want obstruction of justice charges on top of everything else?

EVERETT: I can't in good conscience bring trouble to the door of a friend.

CONSTABLE: Seems trouble has already found you both.

[*Pause.* EVERETT *has become a bit detached; he looks around the room as if everything is unreal.*]

Have you been drinking, Mr. Klippert?

EVERETT: No sir.

CONSTABLE: Is what I am saying putting you to sleep? I don't feel I have your full attention.

EVERETT: I was thinking of *A Touch of Evil.* I saw it at the Chinook Drive-In. Orson Welles and Marlene Dietrich. Really terrific; did you see it?

CONSTABLE: Is the drive-in cinema a place you frequent?

EVERETT: Why sure, everyone loves the pictures. Don't you?

CONSTABLE: My habits are not in question here.

EVERETT: Orson Welles as Captain Quinlan says to Marlene Dietrich as Tana:

Come on, read my future for me.
You haven't got any, she replies.
What do you mean, he asks?
Your future's all used up …

CONSTABLE: Is this going somewhere, Mr. Klippert?

EVERETT: It's just—you ever get the feeling you tumbled into a movie somehow?

CONSTABLE: I can't say as I have.

EVERETT: [*snaps*] If we're in a detective movie right now, you must be the bad cop. [*points to the door*] So the good cop will be here any minute with my coffee and sandwich, right?

CONSTABLE: That how you want to play this?

[CONSTABLE *puts his head down, starts to write on a ledger.*]

EVERETT: I surely don't mean any disrespect. I've just never had any dealings with the law. Never had any reason to.

[*EVERETT is silent. He puts his head down.* CONSTABLE *slaps a paper down on the desk.*]

CONSTABLE: I have here a complaint. A father and upstanding member of this city states that you have been harassing his son.

EVERETT: Harassing?

CONSTABLE: I have a sworn duty to protect the young men of this city from you and others of your … ilk. To protect them from debauchery.

[*EVERETT is silent; his head hangs down.*]

EVERETT: I never hurt anyone, I swear to you. But I confess I don't know what debauchery means—

CONSTABLE: The hell you don't. Corruption. Perversion. Do I make myself clear?

[*EVERETT has his head in his hands, he shakes his head "no, no, no" through the next part.*]

Are you a sodomist?

EVERETT: No!

CONSTABLE: What about gross indecency? That ring a bell? Do you know it's against the law?

EVERETT: I am not a man who studies the law—

CONSTABLE: That's pretty damn convenient. What about the word pedophile? Do you know what that means?

[*EVERETT is buffeted by the words: he cannot seem to bring his head up or fight for himself.*]

Let me bring you up to speed. A pedophile, Mr. Klippert, is someone who sexually molests children.

EVERETT: Children, no! I would *never*—please, I never ever hurt anyone. I never did force anyone …

CONSTABLE: Force anyone? To do what?

EVERETT: Please!

[*The* CONSTABLE *takes a little black book out of his pocket and drops it with a thud in front of* EVERETT.]

CONSTABLE: And what do we have here?

EVERETT: My address book.

[*After letting the book have its impact, the* CONSTABLE *picks it up and reads.*]

CONSTABLE: Theodore Wilmot. 185 Fourth Avenue. Shall I go by and see what Theo has to say for himself?

EVERETT: He's my friend.

CONSTABLE: William Bowmore … maybe bring him down to the station for a chat. And what's this name right here. I can't read your hand writing. It starts with an H-a-

EVERETT: No, please.

CONSTABLE: There are … a lot of names in here. [*Shakes his head*] We are in the midst of an epidemic, but no one wants to hear it.

[CONSTABLE *stares Everett down with evident disgust.*]

The men listed here. Did you touch them in their private parts?

EVERETT: Not … everyone. Some are my relatives, some are my friends!

CONSTABLE: Not everyone. But some. Which of the men in this little black book participated with you in these … acts?

EVERETT: [*quietly*] If I tell you …

CONSTABLE: What's that? You'll need to speak up, Mr. Klippert.

EVERETT: If I tell you what you want to know about me … will you promise to leave the others in peace?

CONSTABLE: This is a criminal investigation. I can't personally promise anything. But you are always better off cooperating with the law. If you were to write a full confession …

[*CONSTABLE slides the clipboard and a pen across the table to Everett. EVERETT's head hangs down. His hair hangs over his face. Very slowly he picks up the pen, looks at it.*]

[*Then EVERETT begins to write.*]

Good decision. We live in a fair and just country Mr. Klippert. Canada isn't some petty tin-can dictatorship.

[*As EVERETT writes and the CONSTABLE paces, we hear Christmas carollers faintly in the street singing: God Rest Ye Merry Gentlemen, Let Nothing Ye Dismay … After a time, the constable takes the board from Everett and reads it.*]

We won't be needing the cuffs, then. Take your time and finish up, we'll get a cell ready for you.

You'll come along quietly.

EVERETT: Now? But I … I have to drive the Christmas bus.

CONSTABLE: I am afraid you won't be driving any bus at all for some time, Mr. Klippert. Christmas or otherwise.

EVERETT: Why not?

CONSTABLE: What you have confessed to is gross indecency under the Criminal Code of Canada. It carries a prison sentence of four years for each count, and you'll remain in custody until a date is set for your trial. With the holidays upon us, that date will take us into the new year.

EVERETT: I'll be in jail for Christmas?

CONSTABLE: Afraid so, Mr. Klippert. No one likes being on the inside over the holidays but we make the best of it. Turkey and all the fixings. The ladies from the church put on a big spread for all the prisoners.

EVERETT: Prisoners. That's what I am now. [*slowly*] A prisoner.

CONSTABLE: Don't take it too hard, son. You did the right thing.

EVERETT: Did I?

[*We hear the carollers again, more clearly from outside. God rest ye, merry gentlemen, let nothing ye dismay … remember Christ our saviour was born on Christmas day …*]

Scene 14
(*monster's hands*)

We hear the sensational background music of the old monster movie.

EVERETT: You like the picture shows? Who doesn't, right?

[*50S MOVIE ANNOUNCER VOICE: "Godzilla, king of the monsters! Surging up through the depths of the sea on a tidal wave of terror to wreak vengeance on mankind. A gigantic beast stalking the earth, crushing all before it in a cyclonic cavalcade of electrifying horror."*]

[*The movie music/announcer fade.*]

In the pictures, anything can happen. Anything in the world. [*beat*] You ever look down at your own hands. Try it now. Familiar, right? [*beat*] "Know it like the back of my hand." We say this about country roads we wandered as a child or hymns or nursery rhymes. Any old thing that you know so well that you can't remember how you learned it first.

[*He holds up his own hands.*]

Have you ever been fingerprinted? It's mighty strange, I don't mind telling you. The policeman takes your hand ever so gently. You can't move during this, you have to hold your breath while he presses each finger first into the ink then onto the blotter, rolling it from one side to the other until he has a full set.

The ink stains your hands for a long time after. A set of fingerprints all by themselves can make it seem like you have done something wrong.

[*He holds his hands out in front of him, looking at them.*]

Your own hands that fits snug into your ball glove. Your hands that can fix things and care for the sick ...

[*He holds his hands out in front, kind of like Godzilla.*]

Well they don't seem like your hands at all. They seem like a monster's hands ...

[*He moves his lips silently, along with the movie announcer.*]

Godzilla, king of the monsters. It's alive! Raging through the streets on a rampage of total destruction. Jet planes cannot destroy it. Bombs cannot kill it. Is this the end of our civilization itself?

[*Lights fade.*]

Scene 15
(*on your flesh*)

MAXINE *and* TONYA *on the picnic table. They have boxes of Chicken on the Way.*

MAXINE: These fritters. Obscenely good.

TONYA: If they bottle this smell, I'll wear it as perfume. So for tonight, I need an icebreaker ...

MAXINE: Your show's tonight?

TONYA: Yeah and I am the "only only" on the ticket again. So I need something to let the audience move past it.

MAXINE: Should they move past it?

TONYA: You need to open the door, if you want to work mainstream audiences. Can't represent all that and still be funny, right?

MAXINE: *You* can.

TONYA: You're biased.

MAXINE: You're brilliant.

TONYA: As long as you think so. Hey when am I going to get to meet the fam, anyway. I'm starting to think you're ashamed of me.

MAXINE: Ashamed of *you*, never. My family on the other hand …

TONYA: What are they? Knuckle-dragging Holocaust deniers? Are you descended from a long line of ogres? What?

MAXINE: They're … well-intentioned. Clueless. They would make polite small talk and feed you a supper of, I am sure, perogies with potatoes and a side of potato perogies.

TONYA: That's harsh.

MAXINE: And say eight cringeworthy things while helping you largely to jellied salad.

TONYA: Babe, that's what family is for. To embarrass you in front of your lover. My ma is wondering if you might not be a figment of my imagination.

MAXINE: Maybe I am. Think about it.

TONYA: I'm pretty sure if you were a fantasy, you'd wear more lingerie and talk a whole lot less.

MAXINE: Tonya, can you stop it?

TONYA: What, mining my personal life for comic gold? Nope.

MAXINE: Why not?

TONYA: Because when I'm not really the one in control. Something or someone takes over …

MAXINE: Well that's … creepy.

TONYA: Creepy, no, it's amazing.

MAXINE: *You* are amazing. [*beat*] But it's just that when you make jokes about us, our personal lives …

TONYA: That's what I'm saying, it's my subconscious at work—

MAXINE: The more accurate term is unconscious, although—

TONYA: Dammit, you promised.

MAXINE: Freud used the German for "sub-" and "un-" interchangeably at first, but then—

TONYA: You promised that if I shacked up with a professor you could turn off the autocorrect. Lies! All lies! There's no off button. No mute. That's the problem with women in general, as a rule of thumb. They never shut up. Not allowed to avail yourself of the duct tape, any more.

[*TONYA weighs this. Is it good material for her act? MAXINE sees what she is doing and reacts with a frown.*]

[*TONYA considers*] Could I use that?

MAXINE: Misogynist *and* violent. Great.

TONYA: Look, how come a dude can make a joke about how the wife isn't giving him any. Or she is, lucky bastard. And wink wink, nudge nudge. We all laugh right along with him?

MAXINE: [*shrugs*] Could it be the unacknowledged continued dominance of heteronormative patriarchal mainstream culture?

TONYA: I want that laugh that dude gets when he tells us all his wife gave him some. Everyone is like … Yeah, Melvin! You go, boy! You went and got yours!

MAXINE: That's so het. So cis. So incredibly sexist that I can't even begin to—[*beat*] Also, who's Melvin?

TONYA: Not important—

MAXINE: Someone from work?

TONYA: He's like "everyman." So I'm like guys, guys, what's your hot tip for when you really need to get some head? What do you do, dip it in Bernard Callebault chocolate? And … nothing. Crickets.

MAXINE: Did you actually make that joke at work—

TONYA: I mean is that something a shift supervisor should write you up for?

MAXINE: Oh, Tonya.

TONYA: Making people laugh is what I was put on this earth to do. When I did my vision quest—

MAXINE: You did a vision quest?

TONYA: No, I did not, Max. But if I crack a joke ... and see just a tiny frigging bit of the ungodly weight shifting from somebody's shoulders ... Well, I think that is why I was put here on this earth.

MAXINE: It's great when it works, but laughter can hurt people too.

TONYA: I'm not talking about the down punch. I want that great cosmic belly laugh. The one that rattles your teeth and shakes your guts! Makes you question everything you know. That is the true medicine, Max.

MAXINE: Wow.

TONYA: So, I ask you: was I put on this earth to sit in a cubicle in a call centre?

[*Beat.*]

MAXINE: Did you get fired, Tonya?

TONYA: Of course not. I quit. I'll get another joe-job, don't sweat it.

MAXINE: I can't help but sweat it. It's what I do: I sweat it.

TONYA: So this ah ... thing I wanted to show you ... We've been seeing each other for ... what ...

MAXINE: Six months. Six months and three days.

TONYA: Right and I wanted to do something special to—ah shit, I'm so bad at this. I wanted to mark that, you know?

MAXINE: This can't be what I think it is? Here, at Chicken on the Way? Ton?

[*TONYA rolls up her sleeve. It is a tattoo, not the engagement ring Maxine was expecting.*]

What is it? The sign for infinity?

TONYA: It's the Métis flag. And here ...

MAXINE: My name.

TONYA: You don't like it, it's too much.

MAXINE: No, it's not that, I …

TONYA: What?

MAXINE: I'm just … processing … I mean you are the sweetest, funniest, wisest, most beautiful woman I have ever laid eyes on—

TONYA: Aw, stop it. [*beat*] Actually, go on …

MAXINE: I mean, you're talented and smart, you drive a motorcycle, and now you have tattooed my *name* on your *flesh*! I am living the lesbian dream.

TONYA: So you *do* like it.

MAXINE: Like it? I love it. I love you, I am—speechless.

[*They embrace, then after a moment,* TONYA *grabs her phone.*]

What are you doing?

TONYA: Calling ma, one sec.

MAXINE: Now?

TONYA: She bet me fifty bucks you'd run away screaming. Ha! Take that, ma.

[TONYA *gathers the remnants of the meal, is dialling her mom.*]

MAXINE: You made a bet …

TONYA: [*on the phone*] Hey ma, whatcha doing? No, no, she liked it …

[MAXINE *is speechless, follows* TONYA *off.*]

Scene 16
(*the next round*)

EVERETT *sits on his bunk; he has a glass half full of water and a letter from his sister.*

EVERETT: My big sister Leah has got to be the most determined person on this earth. We lost our mother when we were children. All I remember is the print of her apron, the softness of it against my cheek. But what you look for in a mother: someone who loves you come what may? I have that in my big sister Leah. She trained as a legal secretary and has filed appeal after appeal on my behalf. She says we must remain optimistic.

[*He pauses and holds up his glass of water.*]

The optimist would tell you this is half full. The pessimist would tell you it's half empty. The politician will promise to fill it to the top if elected. The cynic wonders who drank the other half ... while the fellows back home would be wondering "Who's buying the next round." What I'd give to be back there with them now.

[*He sips, thinks. Picks up a letter.*]

[*He reads from her letter.*]

Dear Everett,

I have great news at last. Mr. William Wuttunee has agreed to take your case. He comes from the Cree people in Saskatchewan. He has battled adversity to become the first Indian lawyer in Western Canada. He is a fine gentleman and champion of his people. I have high hopes that he can finally force some action on your appeal.

[*He puts the letter down, picks up the glass again.*]

I tell you what. We should all be so lucky to have such people in our corner. Glass half full it is. [*raises the glass in a toast*] Here's to my sister Leah and Mr. William Wuttunee.

[*Drinks the rest and places the glass down as the lights fade.*]

Scene 17
(*trouble to the door*)

Crossfade to MAXINE *and* HANDSOME *in the senior's residence. "God Rest Ye Merry Gentlemen"—the Muzak version—is playing faintly. A couple seasonal items (potted poinsettia, a snow globe) adorn his room.*

MAXINE: Incredible that police at that time would detain people and question them without just cause—

HANDSOME: You counted yourself lucky if *all* you got were questions.

MAXINE: Did it happen to you?

HANDSOME: They put me in the back of a squad car one time. But I talked my way out.

MAXINE: How?

HANDSOME: Told them I was new in town and got lost. They warned me about the queers lurking in that area. I … said nothing. But Everett was a different story. I always think of him at this time of the year. He was supposed to drive the Christmas bus.

MAXINE: They set his bail at $9000.

HANDSOME: So much money back then. How many times I wish I could have gone back in time and paid it for him.

MAXINE: Originally a ten-year sentence, but according to the timeline I've pieced together he was released after five for good behaviour.

HANDSOME: That's Everett for you. Chased up a tree by a lion, he'd still admire the view. He was just so damn good … you know? He did the right thing, and not to impress people. It came from inside. And he took the hit for all of us. Took it right on the nose.

MAXINE: How do you mean?

HANDSOME: Cops wanted him to name us. He wouldn't.

MAXINE: He pled guilty to protect you?

HANDSOME: He said he couldn't in good conscience …

EVERETT: I can't in good conscience …

HANDSOME/EVERETT: … bring trouble to the door of a friend.

MAXINE: That's brave.

HANDSOME: Yes and jail ... for a guy like him. He ... suffered in there.

MAXINE: I can imagine. And when he got out, he left to work up north. Do you know why?

HANDSOME: He wanted to leave all this behind. He wanted a fresh start. But they wouldn't let him have it.

MAXINE: So you saw him before he left town?

HANDSOME: Yes I did.

[*HANDSOME gets up from the table and crosses over to:*]

Scene 18
(*strongbox of your heart*)

An alleyway in the downtown.

EVERETT: Well now, haven't you come up in the world.

HANDSOME: Managing a crew. Hard work, but I like it.

EVERETT: Looks good on you.

HANDSOME: Thanks. [*beat*] Listen, I got your letters. I should have written back.

EVERETT: That's alright Handsome. I didn't have much for news. Prison is nothing to write home about.

HANDSOME: Was it ... terrible. I should have visited, I—

EVERETT: It's no place to spend your free time. Don't fret, now.

[*EVERETT puts a hand gently on Handsome's cheek, briefly.*]

Let's just put it in the rearview, shall we?

[*HANDSOME looks to the right and left to see if anyone is watching them.*]

HANDSOME: That's for the best. Now Everett, I'm going to give you some advice and you can take it or leave it, just as you see fit.

EVERETT: What's that?

HANDSOME: Find yourself a wife. A good woman who will give you the space you need to keep a little bit of life ... for yourself. Who will keep the house and look after the children—

EVERETT: A wife? But what about ...

[*EVERETT puts his hand on Handsome's arm. HANDSOME covers it gently with his own briefly before stepping back.*]

HANDSOME: You can't be a man without one. You can't let these feelings control you. You have to take all these stormy and powerful feelings ...

[*HANDSOME reaches for Everett, pulls him into the dark of the alley. EVERETT resists for moment, then relents. We hear their ragged breathing in the darkness. We see the silhouettes of their bodies.*]

And you carve out a little portion of your life where you can feel. Like this.

EVERETT: I can't ...

HANDSOME: Do you want me to stop?

EVERETT: No, please ... don't ... stop.

HANDSOME: You find a little corner of the world where you can be free. And when it's over, you take all those feelings and you lock them up tight in a strongbox.

[*We hear EVERETT's breathing in the dark as he climaxes.*]

The strongbox is your heart. Then you go and find yourself a smart woman—a woman who knows which way the wind is blowing—and settle down.

[*There is a silence. The city lights twinkle. The men compose themselves.*]

Listen, I'm sorry, I shouldn't have said what I said to you before.

EVERETT: What's that?

HANDSOME: About not being … like you.

EVERETT: Why not, if it's what you believe?

HANDSOME: You got to find a way to play the hand you've been dealt.

EVERETT: Pretty bad hand, Handsome. Maybe we should pitch it in?

HANDSOME: This is the way the world is. You got to toughen up, learn how to take a punch or these guys out here, they'll eat you alive.

EVERETT: I got a lesson or two in taking a punch on the inside.

HANDSOME: Maybe learn to throw one then.

[*Cuffs Everett upside the head.*]

Come on.

EVERETT: You won't make me do it, Handsome.

HANDSOME: No?

EVERETT: Nothing I want bad enough to raise my hand against my fellow man.

HANDSOME: [*cuffs him again, playful but a bit too hard*] You sure about that?

EVERETT: Quit it now.

HANDSOME: Nothing at all in this world you want bad enough to fight for?

[*EVERETT grabs him; there is a small tussle.*]

You can have me. Right here, right now. Would you fight for that?

EVERETT: In the dark.

HANDSOME: A poor offering, but I'm all I've got to give.

EVERETT: I'll take it.

[*Lights fade.*]

Scene 19
(*in the noodle*)

MAXINE is working on her computer in their kitchen. TONYA comes in.

TONYA: How's our Mr. Klippert this morning?

MAXINE: I have here a new box of his letters that were stored in his great-niece's attic. I have to get them back to the family by Monday. From what I can tell he was the sweetest, most honest man on this great wide prairie … which led directly to his downfall.

TONYA: Like you.

MAXINE: Nah. Each time he stuck out his hand in friendship: they slapped cuffs on it.

TONYA: He bought into the system.

MAXINE: Oh that's what you mean: "like me." I don't buy into the system.

TONYA: No?

MAXINE: I am trying to change it, but I don't buy *into* it—

TONYA: Alright, alright. Make you a sandwich?

MAXINE: Not hungry.

[*TONYA heads into the kitchen. MAXINE returns to her work, reading from Everett's diaries and journals. EVERETT is illuminated in his jail cell and he is playing a game of patience with a deck of cards.*

EVERETT: Somebody smart once said there are nine things you need to be happy. [*he counts these off as he plays cards*]. Health enough to support your needs. Wealth enough to support your needs. Strength to battle when difficulties arise. Grace to confess your sins. Patience to toil until some good comes of it. Charity to see some good in your neighbour. Love enough to move you to be helpful to others. Faith to make real the things of God. And last but not least … hope for the future.

[*He puts the last card away. He has won.*]

[*EVERETT taps his head*] Prison. Is all in the noodle. You have to keep the possibility alive that the next minute, the one after this one … could be a good one.

[*MAXINE does not hear him, but seems to take this in, somehow. There are newspaper clippings about Everett fastened to a cork board above her work station. On one of them is a picture of him. MAXINE speaks to it.*]

MAXINE: You refused to be ashamed. Kept on finding ways to be happy, no matter what they threw at you.

[*TONYA comes back in with a sandwich at the tail end of this.*]

TONYA: I swear I am starting to get jealous.

[*TONYA embraces her from behind. MAXINE acknowledges the embrace, but does not fully give in to it.*]

MAXINE: You are jealous of a man.

TONYA: A bit.

MAXINE: A dead, gay man.

TONYA: He's getting more attention than me.

MAXINE: That's a stretch even for the super duper jealousy powers of the Modern Urban Lesbian. So when he finally gets out of jail he marries a woman, refuses to talk to anyone about his life before. He could have been a hero, a spokesman …

TONYA: You can't make him into the icon you want him to be. Oh poor Max, pull all the microfiche you want, you just can't tidy up this fucking messy world.

MAXINE: Why?

TONYA: Why? Because people, for the most part, suck. And I'm not just talking your people. Want to know who hurt me the most for being gay? My people. Now, why would that be.

MAXINE: You only hurt the ones you love.

TONYA: That's a maxim, Maxine.

[*TONYA releases Maxine, pouting a bit.*]

MAXINE: I have blown this deadline twice. If I don't have a publication before year-end review.

TONYA: Fifteen minutes, we'll go for the land speed record. I guarantee you, you will see the whole world in an entirely different light.

MAXINE: Sex isn't some magic button you push that just makes all your problems disappear.

TONYA: What are you talking about, that's exactly what sex is! [*beat*] I mean I know this job is, like, *important* and all …

MAXINE: Ten years living like a student, squinting over microfiche and eating Mr. Noodle. If I don't get this position … I'm stale bread at the bakery. No one else will want me.

TONYA: Don't say that.

MAXINE: My skills are useless in the real world, I have no clue what else I could be—

TONYA: Max.

MAXINE: What?

TONYA: You can be Max. Who loves old things. And Weetabix with honey in the morning, and vinyl records, and me—right?

MAXINE: Yes, but—

TONYA: No job can change that. I mean why do you do all this? Is it just a fetish for white gloves and special collections?

MAXINE: White gloves aren't used anymore, actually. The bleach in the cotton is worse for documents than human hands—

TONYA: Or for the librarians who wear them.

MAXINE: I may have had a penchant for librarians—

TONYA: Fetish!

MAXINE: Technically, a fetish would be for the object … whereas a fascination with a whole person or activity would be a kink—

[*TONYA grabs a pillow, threatens to hit her.*]

In the past, the distant past! But that's not why I keep going back to the archive.

TONYA: Why, then?

MAXINE: Fear, basically. Historians are a very fearful people. You spend years soaking up information. Letters, newspaper clippings, court documents ... you piece together a narrative ... but then everything can be dynamited by one piece of paper. [*gestures to the box*] Or by something that an elderly gentleman tells you over tea.

TONYA: That's amazing.

MAXINE: No, it's terrifying, it's crippling.

TONYA: When I need guidance, I go to the Elders.

MAXINE: Wisdom isn't really my family's deal. They're more into ... elbow grease and gin rummy.

TONYA: Not your blood family. Handsome, he's your Queer Elder.

[*Beat.*]

MAXINE: Isn't it appropriation, though, to use that term?

TONYA: Settlers are hilarious. Worry yourselves sick about using the wrong word. But when it comes to huge land grabs? Scooping up natural resources? No problem.

MAXINE: I fully accept the implication that comes with my position ... but I rankle at being lumped in with the settlers constantly.

TONYA: Oh, do you rankle? Seems dangerous. What happens when you rankle?

[*TONYA tries again to hold Maxine; MAXINE keeps working.*]

Look, how do I say this? It's like some part of you is always some-place else—

MAXINE: That's not true.

EVERETT: Got to find a way to play the hand you've been dealt.

TONYA: It's like you always …

EVERETT/TONYA: … take your feelings and lock them away.

MAXINE: Please don't say that; I'm right here.

TONYA: Physically yes. But you, the real you—your spirit—you keep it locked away in …

TONYA *overlapping with* EVERETT: … some kind of strongbox.

TONYA: And it's hard to be … on the outside of that, you know?

MAXINE: This week is such a logjam. Exams and papers … There are so many hoops to jump through right now.

TONYA: But … there's always going to be another hoop. Just like there's a reason you won't tell your family about me. Or your colleagues at work. Or any of your friends. Maybe you're not even gay, Max. You think about that? Maybe I'm just a pit stop for you.

MAXINE: Don't say that.

TONYA: You've just pulled in for a lube job to get you ready for your shiny new life. A nice cushy job, find a nice enlightened dude to marry, and settle down.

MAXINE: That's a cheap shot and it's not true.

TONYA: Then why are you ashamed of me.

MAXINE: I'm not ashamed of *you*, it's just—

TONYA: Just what? Oh never mind.

[*TONYA grabs her jacket. Heads for the door.*]

MAXINE: Where are you going?

TONYA: To the club for a bit, I have a gig. You probably forgot, but that's fine.

[*Lights fade.*]

Scene 20
(*legislating love*)

MAXINE and HANDSOME in his room.

MAXINE: How old did you say you are now?

HANDSOME: A gentleman never tells and a lady never asks.

MAXINE: [*smiles*] I do need to know, though. To resolve a couple conflicts in my timeline.

HANDSOME: You and your fucking timeline.

MAXINE: [*carefully*] You met in 1960 or a little before, is that correct?

HANDSOME: What are you trying to insinuate? You got something to ask, just spit it out.

MAXINE: I am trying to get a fulsome picture of your life and Mr. Klippert's—

HANDSOME: Life was the shits! There's a fulsome picture for you. THE SHITS. Put that down in your report. Several times, underlined in block letters, full stop.

MAXINE: Look, you're not feeling well—

HANDSOME: I am not feeling well because I am fucking dying.

MAXINE: I could come back tomorrow.

HANDSOME: Might be dead tomorrow. Your call.

[*MAXINE hesitates, but does not leave. After a moment.*]

You're still here.

MAXINE: Yup.

HANDSOME: Sit.

[*She does.*]

What do you want to know.

MAXINE: How old were you?

HANDSOME: Why?

MAXINE: I got a … phone call … from someone who said that Mr. Klippert …

HANDSOME: It's not true. I was a man. I knew what I was doing.

MAXINE: Did he give you money?

HANDSOME: Yes, if I needed it. And dinner if I needed that too. He was—you wouldn't understand this—someone you could count on. The other guys knew it too. But this was a different time. You think because I was younger than him that he took advantage, he "made me gay."

MAXINE: Of course I don't think that.

HANDSOME: Well he didn't. I wanted the experience and he showed me kindness, taught me things. Why is it that when a man does this for a younger woman it's just fine?

MAXINE: I'm not judging you.

HANDSOME: Look, you're the historian … has the law ever been able to deal with love?

MAXINE: Were you … Handsome, were you in love with Mr. Klippert?

HANDSOME: [beat] We didn't carve our initials in tree trunks. Didn't walk hand in hand by the river …

MAXINE: No …

HANDSOME: You make a separation. Family over here. Work over here. Forget living together, sharing a home, meals. You give pleasure, you receive it, that's it: that's all we queers get.

MAXINE: But we can get married now; that makes a difference.

[Pause.]

HANDSOME: You make me laugh, running off to the suburbs to get hitched and make babies—

MAXINE: That's somewhat harsh …

HANDSOME: Harsh? What do you know about harsh? What are you after, exactly? Some findings. Some foregone conclusion to fill in the blank space on your paper.

MAXINE: I'm trying to understand. But how can I when you don't want to tell me anything. Or nothing I can print!

HANDSOME: Not everyone likes to be in the limelight. I wanted to live a quiet life.

MAXINE: You hid. And you told Everett to do the same thing.

HANDSOME: You want some version that walls you off from the past. Mark a point in time and say that was then, this is now. But you know what? There is nothing in the past to save. People's lives were torn apart. They died in shame.

MAXINE: I understand … that's why we fought for the apology and the pardon—

HANDSOME: And you want to come here and take my story and put it down on paper to … make yourself feel better.

MAXINE: No, that's not what I—

HANDSOME: Well I won't do it. He's gone. Don't you get it. Dead. I'm mostly dead—

MAXINE: I'm sorry.

HANDSOME: Sorry sorry sorry. All these fucking apologies are just too late.

[*HANDSOME puts his head down. Is he crying? MAXINE moves to comfort him; he shakes her off.*]

I'm not a part of this. I'm not a proper queer anyway.

MAXINE: There's no one definition—

HANDSOME: None of this means shit to me. Go on now, get out of here.

[*MAXINE stands but doesn't leave.*]

MAXINE: It's just that I had something … not something for the study, something personal to ask you—

HANDSOME: Well spit it out then.

MAXINE: But now I—this isn't the right time. I can't.

HANDSOME: Of course you can't. You're a mouse of a person. And this is a stupid thing to be wasting time on.

[*MAXINE looks like she might have a reply, but then:*]

Go on, get out of here.

[*MAXINE turns and flees.*]

[*Blackout.*]

Scene 21
(*a live one*)

TONYA is onstage, performing stand-up. EVERETT is facing the other way, in silhouette eating popcorn in the glow of the TV screen. As before, he may react in an understated way. Shake his head, slap his knee, etc. He would be watching something like Johnny Carson … we may hear a distant ripple of the laugh track or the "badum tish" of the high hat after a joke. The sound is bleeding across from the 1960s to now. It might have a slight ripple in it and should not "hit the nose" in terms of telling us how to feel about Tonya's performance. It should add a layer/remind us of the passage of time.

TONYA: Lesbians. I am so tired of them. Somebody tell me what is it with lesbians and their cats? No more than three, ladies. There is a cut off. I swear if I have to listen to one more story about the skin ailments of the long-haired tabby, I'm going to cut someone. And potlucks. Lesbians and their potlucks. Can we just visit each other without leaving a trail of hummus and bean casserole?

[*Beat.*]

Any queers in the audience, this evening? Your family cool with it? [*TONYA listens and reacts to the responses*] My ma is pretty down with me being a dyke. "So you're into the beaver, not the stag, no biggie." But recently I had to break it to her that I wasn't just dating a woman … I was dating a white woman.

And you know what she says? "Make sure she's good in the sack, 'cause based on personal experience … Pfft." [*thumbs down motion*]

And she heads off to Bingo.

[*MAXINE has been watching and drinking. The empty shot glasses are lined up on the table.*]

And she's right to be afraid for me. You've heard of Lesbian Bed Death, right? If you haven't, it is about as desirable as a mosquito infestation in a malaria zone. And as common. Brothers and sisters of all stripes, no matter where you like to poke it or have it poked … Do not let bed death happen to you. HEED ME!

MAXINE: Bravo, bravo.

TONYA: Uh oh. We got a live one.

[*TONYA looks out over the audience, realizes it is Maxine heckling her.*]

Hey everyone, meet my old lady. I bring her along to heckle me at all my shows.

MAXINE: White girls in bed! Hilarious. Bartender! [*holds up her glass*]

TONYA: She's cut off. Although it is refreshing to see a white person drunk and disorderly in public for a change. Seriously, I wasn't talking about you, babe. [*points at Maxine, speaks to the crowd*] Total wildcat in the sack, folks.

MAXINE: Oh, it's *not* me …

[*Pause.*]

TONYA: We're doing this?

MAXINE: That's a relief!

TONYA: Here? For real?

MAXINE: Oh just a *different* white girl who sucks in bed.

TONYA: Alright then. So I'm seeing a teacher. Anyone here knocking boots with a teacher? It's kind of taxing, right? They correct your grammar, have rebuttals for everything. Never. Shut. Up. But there are perks, too. It's nice to meet a teacher who doesn't beat me and make me sit in a corner. She didn't steal me from my parents or anything, so I guess I shouldn't complain. [*pause*] White people, hey?

MAXINE: You can't—you can't do that.

[*MAXINE stands up.*]

TONYA: Do what?

MAXINE: If I said: "you people" ...

TONYA: You'd be a racist, imperialist bigot.

MAXINE: Exactly!

TONYA: We've had the shitty end of the stick since you got here and went all genocide-y on us. So we get the moral high ground. Want to swap?

Oh, that smarts. So hard to find the G-spot, isn't it guys? Seriously. But when you find it, you just know. [*beat*] That one spot thing is a myth, by the way. Like Columbus finding the "new world." There are like five different zones, each with their own sensitivities. It's complicated, I know. I feel your pain.

[*MAXINE has had it; she runs out.* TONYA *sees Maxine has left.*]

I think ... I just got dumped. Before a live audience, ladies and gentlemen. Sorry, that was too binary, I mean gentlefolk. Was that a first here at the Laf Rack? Yes? Yes! I think I'll leave it at that. I have to be getting home and start loading all my stuff back into the U-Haul. Thanks, you've been a great audience. [*beat*] They tell us to say that at the end, no matter what happens.

[*She bows, says "thanks" as the lights fade.*]

Scene 22

(*how far north*)

EVERETT and HANDSOME sit on a construction site.

EVERETT: Lady answered when I called last time.

HANDSOME: Yes. That was my wife.

EVERETT: She sounded nice.

HANDSOME: You surprised?

EVERETT: Not really. "You can't be a man without one" after all.

HANDSOME: Look, I said some things—

EVERETT: No point worrying about yesterday. Yesterday worries about itself and each day has enough trouble of its own, don't you think? [*beat*] No hard feelings. Your wife doesn't mind … that you come down here?

HANDSOME: We have an understanding.

EVERETT: Good thing to have. Precious little of that in the world.

HANDSOME: She's a good woman. Maybe has a whole world of feeling inside her too, for all I know. So we understand one another. We share the cost of things, the household, the burden. There's something else we have together too. That I didn't tell you last time.

EVERETT: What's that?

HANDSOME: Kids. Two. A boy and a girl.

EVERETT: Wow. [*claps him on the shoulder*] That's … wow, that's really swell. Are they happy and healthy?

HANDSOME: They are.

EVERETT: I'm so pleased for you. Truly I am. [*beat*] And so glad I have a chance to congratulate you before I leave town.

HANDSOME: Where are you going?

EVERETT: Up north.

HANDSOME: North, how far?

EVERETT: As far as I can get. Past the North Pole and the icebergs and the polar bears.

HANDSOME: What you going to do up there?

EVERETT: I saw an ad in the paper. Mining company in the Northwest Territories needs a mechanic's helper.

HANDSOME: So cold up there.

EVERETT: Well there's cold and then there's cold, you know.

HANDSOME: You could get a job here in the city.

EVERETT: I'm looking for a fresh start too.

HANDSOME: That … makes sense.

EVERETT: Tell you this. From now on, if they ask me "are you a homosexual," I am going to stand up tall. I am going to say "Yes I am a homosexual; how about you?"

HANDSOME: My friend, you can't do that.

EVERETT: If you are ashamed of yourself? If you drop your eyes and cower before a bully. You know what happens? He hits you harder. Learned that lesson on the inside.

HANDSOME: Trust you to find the bright side of prison.

EVERETT: And that's about all it taught me.

HANDSOME: All that time. How did you do it.

EVERETT: Every morning I'd wake up and find myself in the same place and say … can this be real? This can't be real.

HANDSOME: Yes.

EVERETT: Like it was one of those bad movies.

HANDSOME: Life is a B movie, sometimes …

EVERETT: But … prison is in the noodle. Some men will stay in prison their whole lives, all the while they walk around free men on the street. Think about that.

HANDSOME: I want to tell you something before you go.

EVERETT: The past is in the past. Don't be sad, now. Remember a smile is happiness that is found right under your nose. [*beat*] Look me up if you ever find yourself up north.

HANDSOME: How would I find you.

EVERETT: Call to me and I will answer you. [*beat*] Or just head on past Santa's workshop. If you get lost ask Rudolph for directions.

HANDSOME: So this is goodbye.

EVERETT: So long. For now anyway.

[*They hold each other for a moment then say goodbye as the lights fade.*]

Scene 23
(*not swans*)

Morning. MAXINE *and* TONYA's *apartment. Maxine is in a bathrobe gazing at the television, which is playing a nature show.*

MAXINE: Ah. You're alive then.

TONYA: Max, can I turn this off.

MAXINE: Wait, wait. Here comes the good part. The mother penguin, returning from the sea, is about to regurgitate half-digested fish for the chick.

TONYA: You've already seen it?

MAXINE: This channel wraps around about every four hours.

TONYA: Want to get some breakfast? Talk?

MAXINE: Not hungry.

TONYA: Come on.

[MAXINE *shakes her head "no." A pause.* TONYA *watches the* TV. *We hear narration about penguins from the nature show.*]

Remember those two male penguins in the zoo? Partnered up to take care of an egg?

MAXINE: Not a novelty. Upwards of 1500 species from mammals have homosexual pairings. Mention this in class we are sure to fall down a wormhole of Darwinist speculation. Because students would rather talk about penguins than social policy.

TONYA: Those two daddy penguins passing the egg back and forth on their feet, so cute though; do you blame them?

MAXINE: I do. Because applying instinct and biology to human society is not only misleading, it's destructive.

TONYA: Did you make your deadline?

MAXINE: Fuck it.

TONYA: Max, it's okay. People fall apart now and then and it doesn't have to be the end of the world.

MAXINE: Except when it is … [*sighs*] Never mind, let's talk about gay penguins.

TONYA: Birds. Fine. Let's talk about birds. There are some—which ones are they, ducks, geese? That mate for life.

MAXINE: I believe you are referring to swans—

TONYA: Okay swans.

MAXINE: But we are not bound together by some essentialist honking biological imperative: find a life form that appeals to you and then proceed to clamp yourself onto it in a deathgrip come what may—

TONYA: You are hard to talk to sometimes, you know that.

MAXINE: Part of my madcap charm? [*sighs*] No. Look, you clearly have something on your mind, so …

TONYA: Okay. You and I … Max, things have not been great the past little while.

MAXINE: Really?

TONYA: People grow, they change shape. Dammit, why does everything that comes out of my mouth right now sound like a cliché?

MAXINE: Because there are a finite number of human disappointments. Just an infinite number of ways to play them out.

TONYA: Intimacy is …

MAXINE: Okay, go on and say it—

TONYA: Say what?

MAXINE: Complicated. I never pictured myself being in one half of a relationship where that word is used.

TONYA: Complex.

MAXINE: Same thing.

TONYA: No—it's just that we haven't … been intimate in a while.

MAXINE: And that's my fault, I'm sure.

TONYA: No, it's not anyone's *fault*.

MAXINE: I work too hard.

TONYA: It's just the feeling between us …

MAXINE: Tonya, I am tired. Just spit it out.

TONYA: I'm trying.

MAXINE: You already dumped me in front of a live audience, what else do you want?

TONYA: I didn't dump you, you dumped me!

MAXINE: It was horrible, talking about our sex life in public, it hurt—

TONYA: Yeah well things hurt, that happens … but you're the one who left. I know it must seem like I pick on you in my act … But academics are such easy targets. So are white people. So are lesbians. So you? The whole package.

MAXINE: That's why you're with me. Great material for your act.

TONYA: At first, maybe. But since then I have discovered your other qualities.

MAXINE: Such as?

TONYA: They're hard to spot right now.

MAXINE: Fuck you.

TONYA: I deserved that.

MAXINE: You are deliberately trying to pick a fight. And for the life of me I cannot …

TONYA: I'm not, I just …

[*Pause.*]

MAXINE: I'm tracking back through the conversation. Texts I sent you last night that didn't get answered. Ducks. Swans. Intimacy. We're not breaking up. [*beat*] Oh, got it, you want to sleep with other people.

TONYA: Babe, I.

MAXINE: Person. One other person.

TONYA: I …

MAXINE: Oh. You did. You already did, last night.

TONYA: I just don't know what is going on with me.

MAXINE: How's that, since I seem to have nailed it. Look, we're not swans, are we? So forget the life we could have built—the children we could have had …

TONYA: Wait, you want to have kids with me? We never discussed—

MAXINE: Want-*ed*. Tense is important here. Who is she?

TONYA: It doesn't matter—

MAXINE: That little shithead with the lopsided hair that works the door? No, I don't want to know.

TONYA: People screw up, Max.

MAXINE: Oxytocin is the chemical lighting up your brain right now. It's more powerful than heroin and I am not going to fight it.

TONYA: I haven't made anything this [*looks around*] solid with anyone before. And I don't want to lose it.

MAXINE: What are you afraid of losing? A drafty two-bedroom rental with a view of an alleyway?

TONYA: No, it's you. It's us. I don't want to break up.

MAXINE: So what? You want to go out and do your shows and fuck girls who come out to see you perform? And then come home to me where I keep the heat and lights on?

TONYA: No.

MAXINE: Only instead of lying to me, because that gives you, I don't know, some kind of moral itch or, you just want to be able to tell me all about it.

TONYA: No, I am trying—

MAXINE: To what, Tonya? Trying to have your cake and eat it too?

TONYA: No, find out what makes me … happy.

MAXINE: Well, banging the bouncer behind my back, apparently—so have at 'er.

TONYA: Look, I've never had sex be so … important before. I've never had it be this make or break thing. Not in my life so far.

MAXINE: What was it, then? What is it?

[EVERETT *has been lying on his bunk with his eyes closed. He opens them for a moment.*]

TONYA: Sometimes sex *is* love, or …

TONYA/EVERETT: … friendship.

MAXINE: Friendship?!

TONYA: Or comfort, or safety.

EVERETT: [*echoes her, as if agreeing*] Safety … comfort.

MAXINE: Well that's just gross, what am I some kind of ratty old blanket?

TONYA: I am trying to turn the corner and trust. A relationship needs that, I know.

MAXINE: I can't do this.

TONYA: I made a mistake.

TONYA/EVERETT: Everyone makes mistakes.

[*MAXINE considers.*]

[EVERETT *drifts back to sleep.*]

MAXINE: [*puts her hand on Tonya's arm where she knows the tattoo is*] You'll have to find someone to take this off. They can do that now, with a laser.

TONYA: I don't want to take it off.

MAXINE: Get someone good, we don't want it to leave a scar.

TONYA: Maxine, please …

MAXINE: Or maybe you do. Something to remember me by.

TONYA: Don't do this.

MAXINE: Get out.

[*Lights fade as* TONYA *exits.*]

Scene 24
(*not my fire*)

A makeshift RCMP *questioning room in Pine Point,* NWT *1965.*

ARMSTRONG: So, here we are then. Take a seat.

EVERETT: This is jail?

ARMSTRONG: Afraid so. They promised me a new dedicated building when I agreed to take this post, but so far … well you work with what you've got.

EVERETT: Looks like someone's house.

ARMSTRONG: It is, it's mine. That room right there does lock. I use it if one of the ruffians from the mine needs to sleep it off. But we don't need to use it. You plan on being any trouble, Mr. Klippert?

EVERETT: I have no plans at all of that, Constable Armstrong.

ARMSTRONG: Glad to hear it. Get you a cuppa?

EVERETT: Much appreciated.

[ARMSTRONG *puts the kettle on.*]

ARMSTRONG: Now I have a few questions to ask you. You know why I brought you in here?

EVERETT: I reckon I got a pretty good idea.

ARMSTRONG: On the matter of the fire that someone has set—

EVERETT: Oh, the fire—

ARMSTRONG: So you know about it?

EVERETT: No.

ARMSTRONG: But you just said "Oh, the fire" as if you knew—

EVERETT: No, I mean I heard of it, but I thought you were going to ask me about something else.

ARMSTRONG: What did you think I was going to ask you about?

[*EVERETT shakes his head. "Not again."*]

EVERETT: No …

ARMSTRONG: Did you or did you not—

EVERETT: No.

ARMSTRONG: Were you or were you not—

EVERETT: No.

ARMSTRONG: Mr. Klippert, you have got to let me do my job, here.

[*Pause. EVERETT raises his head. He looks into Armstrong's eyes. Considers …*]

Well?

EVERETT: You can call me Everett. I didn't set the fire, but it won't matter.

ARMSTRONG: Are you fooling with me?

EVERETT: I am surely not.

ARMSTRONG: I hope not. Because anything less than cooperation on your part—

EVERETT: I understand.

ARMSTRONG: Someone in your position surely wants to help us get to the truth.

EVERETT: My position.

ARMSTRONG: Sometimes we move to a new place, we think we've left our past behind.

I have pulled up your record and … there are some serious charges here.

[*EVERETT is silent. It is happening again.*]

I can't put this together. On the one hand I have you, the man in front of me who seems decent. Manager at the mine says you are a stand up fellow. They tell me you play shortstop on the company ball team. You eat dinner at their house. Supposedly, you're just a regular guy.

EVERETT: You got me. A regular guy. That's all I ever wanted to be.

ARMSTRONG: On the one hand, I have these folks who vouch for you. And on the other hand, I have these charges. [*pause*] I am kind of missing something here. Can you help me son? I need to connect the dots. Now your family might be able to shed some light—

EVERETT: My family? [*begins to stand*] Please, you haven't called my family.

ARMSTRONG: Sit down, son.

EVERETT: You can't, please.

ARMSTRONG: We'll get to that. Now: Sit. Down.

[*EVERETT sits. Head in hands.*]

So from the top. Your fire—

EVERETT: Not my fire.

ARMSTRONG: The fire you claim you did not start.

EVERETT: Okay.

ARMSTRONG: You do understand that arson is a serious matter. Destruction of private property in excess of five thousand dollars.

EVERETT: I understand. But I didn't do it.

ARMSTRONG: You didn't do it?

EVERETT: No. [*pause*] Sir.

ARMSTRONG: You sure? Arson is a serious thing, to be sure. But if it were me, I might prefer having that on my record …

EVERETT: I did not start the fire.

ARMSTRONG: Maybe not, but I smell smoke. Mind telling me why you chose to come up here? To Pine Point.

EVERETT: I saw an ad in the newspaper for a mechanic's helper. I came up here to the north and I work twelve hours, fourteen hours. I do whatever's needed and I don't complain.

ARMSTRONG: [*surveys paper*] All well and good, but this is an investigation not a job interview.

EVERETT: You can call my boss, at the nickel nine. He'll vouch for me.

ARMSTRONG: And what have you done for him that would cause him to stick his neck out for you?

EVERETT: No, no. It's not like that. I eat dinner with his family.

ARMSTRONG: So I hear. I spoke with his wife.

EVERETT: They have been very kind to me.

ARMSTRONG: They let you babysit their children.

EVERETT: Yes, I come from a big family and I love children—

ARMSTRONG: Is that a fact … [*writing*] And when did you say this began?

[*ARMSTRONG writing on ledger.*]

EVERETT: What are you writing? Please, don't write anything bad. I love children. In the ordinary way, the normal way.

ARMSTRONG: As opposed to what, exactly?

EVERETT: You're getting this all wrong.

ARMSTRONG: Help me get it right, then. What were you arrested for down in Calgary, exactly?

EVERETT: Past the North Pole, past Santa Claus, even. But you can't ever go far enough away. [*to the audience*] I should have been an astronaut. Maybe the moon would be far enough.

[*He has closed his eyes for a moment. We hear, faintly, the moon landing for a moment in the distance.*]

ARMSTRONG: So you work at the mine. Everett! You with me?

EVERETT: Sorry, yes. I am thirsty and just so tired. Can I bother you for a drink of water?

[*ARMSTRONG pours him water.*]

ARMSTRONG: We'll start from the beginning. Where did you work in Calgary?

EVERETT: In the dairy at first but then I got my dream job.

ARMSTRONG: And what was that?

EVERETT: I drive the bus on the downtown route. Calgary Transit operator at your service.

ARMSTRONG: Don't try that. You know quite well we're not in Calgary.

EVERETT: No. I know that.

ARMSTRONG: You're in Pine Point, Northwest Territories.

EVERETT: Yes, I understand.

[*EVERETT speaks to the audience for a moment.*]

Sometimes I catch glimpses in the rearview mirror. Of how life could have been. Would you believe that I can tell just about everything about a man by the way he lets his body down onto the seat of my bus? I can tell if he's going home to a hot dinner, a warm loving family. Or a cold plate in a rented walk-up? Now the rule book that says: a city transit driver may not delay the schedule of the bus to accommodate a single passenger.

ARMSTRONG: Mr. Klippert—

EVERETT: You won't believe it but I can read your life by studying the whites of your knuckles. See who you've loved in the crinkles around your eyes. I should pull away … But have you ever seen, *really* seen the way someone with nowhere to go drops their body onto a seat? Fire me if you have to, but I won't do it.

[*Pause. ARMSTRONG tries again.*]

ARMSTRONG: Excuse me?

EVERETT: Sorry, I kind of floated away there for a moment.

ARMSTRONG: Do that a lot, do you?

EVERETT: Sometimes.

ARMSTRONG: Why do you think that is?

EVERETT: People in my mind's eye … how I imagine them. Are just a whole lot kinder than in real life.

ARMSTRONG: That a fact? I am starting to understand you, Everett. The fact is I don't think any of this is your fault.

EVERETT: You don't …

ARMSTRONG: A lot of men I know would want you wiped off the face of the earth. But I don't feel this way. I think we have to look at this as a sickness.

EVERETT: I'm not sick. I don't feel sick.

ARMSTRONG: Not in the usual way, son. With this kind of sickness … this is all to do with your childhood. You might be sick and not even feel … you might not even know you are sick. We just want to get you some help.

EVERETT: You want to help me?

ARMSTRONG: Yes, to get your head right and live a normal life.

EVERETT: Why did you pick me up?

ARMSTRONG: For suspicion of arson.

EVERETT: Did someone … someone told you I was coming up here, didn't they?

ARMSTRONG: Should they have?

[*Pause, EVERETT does not answer.*]

Mr. Klippert!

EVERETT: Alright.

ARMSTRONG: Would you say that you had any proclivity toward fire as a child?

EVERETT: Not that I remember.

ARMSTRONG: Did you wet the bed as a boy?

EVERETT: No. Why do people keep asking me that?

ARMSTRONG: There is a well-documented link between bed wetting and fire setting. Tormenting small animals and murder. You ever bother animals?

EVERETT: Of course not!

ARMSTRONG: Sodomy and pedophilia. We are trained to detect all of these patterns in human behaviour. [*pause*] We will need to contact your family—

EVERETT: No, please don't involve my family. Is there any way to keep them out of it?

ARMSTRONG: There might be. There just might be. Now, I am only trying to help you. I have held off these dogs as long as I can. I am going to ask you one more time: can you be sure that you never wet the bed as a youngster.

EVERETT: I—

ARMSTRONG: Not even one time.

EVERETT: I am so tired, I …

ARMSTRONG: Did you wet the bed, son? Did you engage in acts of gross indecency with boys in this town? If you cooperate, I can ask the judge to be lenient.

EVERETT: Younger men, yes, but not boys, never boys—

ARMSTRONG: Young men, then? I am just trying to get to the truth. To sort this all out.

EVERETT: All I ever did was to feel … something. Do you understand? I never hurt anyone.

ARMSTRONG: The life you lead. It can't be easy.

EVERETT: No, life … has not been a cakewalk so far.

ARMSTRONG: Here's what I think: inside you there is a decent, clean, good fellow. Who wants to make a clean break of it. Maybe you write this confession. And then we get you the help you need.

[*He slides a clipboard over.*]

EVERETT: You want to … help me.

ARMSTRONG: Why sure, that's why I got into this racket. I might spend the majority of my time waiting for drunks to sleep it off and busting up bare-knuckle brawls ... but now and then you get to make a difference.

[*EVERETT begins to write. ARMSTRONG reads a few words over his shoulder.*]

Chin up, now. Times have changed. You won't be tossed in jail to rot. We are going to rehabilitate you. We can address the root causes of the unnatural act itself.

EVERETT: Unnatural. Funny you should say that because that's just the trouble. Imagine for yourself that you were being asked to touch a man, rather than a woman. It would feel—

ARMSTRONG: Wrong.

EVERETT: Yes, that is how it feels for me ... to touch a woman. Can you understand that?

ARMSTRONG: I understand. Go on ...

[*Lights fade on them, then come up on EVERETT in a spot:*]

EVERETT: I never felt sick. Other than a round of chicken pox and a head cold I really can't say I ever felt sick. But the priests, the police, the judges, the doctors. Over the years I must have talked to a hundred respected men. They all tell me the same thing. I am sick but there is a chance to get better.

[*Pause, we hear echoes of the Godzilla monster music.*]

Scene 25
(*man on the moon*)

EVERETT sits on his bunk in jail. It is August 1969 (Bill C-150 has taken effect).

WILLIAM WUTTUNEE *is on the other end of an old rotary phone. He wears a large, well-cut jacket and has the manner of one who has spent a lifetime fighting the status quo.*

EVERETT: [*on the phone*] Good day Mr. Wuttunee. I just wanted to say thank you for all that you've done for me so far.

WUTTUNEE: We haven't gained much ground, Mr. Klippert, despite the tireless work of your sister Leah and my own best efforts.

EVERETT: Still, it's not every man who wants to take my case.

WUTTUNEE: The way I see it, we need to help one another.

EVERETT: Yes, I have always thought so too. And I do appreciate it.

WUTTUNEE: I wish I were calling you today with better news.

EVERETT: But the prime minister himself said it. I heard it on the TV: "There is no place for the state …

WUTTUNEE: [*finishes for him*] … in the bedrooms of the nation," yes. But I have called today with good news and bad news. Which do you want to hear first?

EVERETT: I think I better have the good news.

WUTTUNEE: The good news is that Bill C-150 has taken effect. Homosexual acts between two adults are no longer criminal in the eyes of the law.

EVERETT: How about that! I wanted to listen to the news, but there's only one television and the fellows won't watch anything but the hockey.

WUTTUNEE: The country has taken a step forward on this issue … if not on so many others.

EVERETT: Can you believe it? I never thought I would see the day, Mr. Wuttunee!

WUTTUNEE: There's more to it, I'm afraid …

EVERETT: You would never think they could put a man on the moon either, but they did it.

WUTTUNEE: The public is entirely on your side. The newspaper stories, editorials, and features. [*reads*] "Gentle Klippert, must he really serve life?" The public wants you to be a free man. But the board of appeals are another matter, I am afraid …

EVERETT: Don't be afraid! It is a brave new world out there.

WUTTUNEE: Your appeal has been denied.

EVERETT: I pictured myself just walking out of here. Like Neil Armstrong and Buzz stepping out in their silver suits …

[*Sounds: crackling sounds of the recording of the moon landing underlaid with some sounds from Stonewall.*]

WUTTUNEE: The law is not retroactive. Your conviction was made before the law was changed … also some charges refer to public acts and so you are …

EVERETT: One small step for man …

WUTTUNEE: In a kind of legal limbo.

EVERETT: One giant leap for mankind. [*beat*] Damn it to hell.

WUTTUNEE: Helluva hard pill to swallow.

EVERETT: How did he think to say that, I wonder. It's a gift, I guess. To know the right thing to say in the right moment.

WUTTUNEE: If it's any consolation everyone out here is pulling for you. You have become something of a figurehead.

EVERETT: I don't want to be a figurehead. I want to be a free man.

[*Silence.* WUTTUNEE *absorbs this and nods his agreement.*]

WUTTUNEE: I understand. I am sorry I could not help you. [*pause*] I could tell you a story about where I grew up. A story about the slow painful process of change. It might not be of any help right now, with your immediate situation …

EVERETT: Well it certainly can't hurt. Go on, please tell me.

WUTTUNEE: What do you have in your hand right now?

EVERETT: A telephone receiver.

WUTTUNEE: Yes. We take it for granted now, but it's kind of a miracle.

EVERETT: Thank you, Mr. Graham Bell.

WUTTUNEE: I saw that my people would need, in the world that was forming around us, to communicate. I asked for telephones to be put in on the reserve. The phone companies told me no, they would not.

EVERETT: Why not?

WUTTUNEE: They told me they would not put in telephones because they did not trust us to pay for them. Then put in a pay phone, I said. And we will pay one nickel at a time. And they did. They put a pay phone in my brother's house. He was the chief at that time. Then I said to them, now give us a light bulb ... and that's how we got services on the reserves. You got to fight for everything, every little thing—

EVERETT: I'm tired, Mr. Wuttunee. And I never was much of a fighter on any account.

WUTTUNEE: I am going to tell you something I don't talk about much. No one expected me to leave the reservation. Let alone finish high school and go to university. But I did. No one expected me to go to law school, nor to become the first Indian to earn a law degree in western Canada, but I did it. I became ... like you, a kind of symbol. I won some cases and I started to make some real changes in the law. Well it was all going really great until I stepped out of line.

EVERETT: What did you do.

WUTTUNEE: I fell in love with the wrong person.

EVERETT: You mean you, too—

WUTTUNEE: Not with a man, but a woman. A white woman. I wasn't put in jail, no, but we could not live together on the reserve.

EVERETT: I am sorry to hear that.

WUTTUNEE: The law is an imperfect instrument and has no idea what to do with love. You can't legislate love. [beat] Now people ask me, will I teach my children to hunt and fish and live off the land like my ancestors did? Will I teach them to speak Cree? [pause] I taught my daughter one song only—my heart song. It is all I can afford.

EVERETT: Real sorry to hear it, Mr. Wuttunee.

WUTTUNEE: And I am damn sorry you aren't a free man today. That is it, Mr. Klippert. Take care of yourself.

EVERETT: And you too, Mr. Wuttunee.

[*Lights fade.*]

Scene 26
(*the next stop*)

MAXINE is on the sofa in her apartment there is a knock at the door. She opens it and HANDSOME enters.

MAXINE: You?

HANDSOME: You have missed two appointments and haven't responded to my messages—

MAXINE: What are you ... are you allowed to be here?

HANDSOME: It's an assisted living complex not a maximum security prison.

MAXINE: How did you get here.

HANDSOME: It's a miracle. I have passed on to the next life and what you see before you is an apparition. [*beat*] The handi-bus stops right outside the complex.

[*He walks past her, looking for the liquor cabinet.*]

Got anything decent to drink in this pigsty.

[*He takes in the state of the apartment.*]

MAXINE: This really isn't a good time.

HANDSOME: Depression. That's what your generation calls this. When things go wrong and you decide to stay in bed. We get pamphlets about it at the residence. Relentless optimism is the order of the day. Express any anti-social tendencies and they'll cart you off to the art gallery, to forest bathing, to goddamn laughing yoga.

MAXINE: There's laughing yoga?

HANDSOME: No word of a lie. Very earnest young man in tights just comes in, starts laughing like a goddamn idiot in front of all of us. Half of us on ventilators the other off their head on meds. You can imagine how that went.

MAXINE: Did it work?

HANDSOME: Well I laughed, but I am not sure it was the right kind of laughter.

MAXINE: A bit on the darker edge.

HANDSOME: The tights saved the experience for me; he was well put together. Just because you're on a diet, doesn't mean you can't look at the menu.

[*MAXINE smiles, finally gestures for him to sit down. He takes in the untidy place, Maxine in her bathrobe.*]

[*EVERETT is on his bunk in a very low light. He may react—again, in an understated way—to some of what transpires.*]

MAXINE: I appreciate that you made the effort to come over here … I'm just …

HANDSOME: You're very busy.

MAXINE: Yes, some things at work … [*she puts her hands in her hair, trailing off*]

HANDSOME: Feeling sorry for oneself is a full-time job. [*beat*] So our … little project, maybe we just call it quits then?

MAXINE: Fine, sure. If that's what you want.

[*Pause; HANDSOME surveys her.*]

HANDSOME: See, there you are. You don't care about the real story. You don't care about Everett or about me.

MAXINE: That's not true.

HANDSOME: This is why I didn't want to talk to you in the first place.

MAXINE: You didn't want to talk to me because you're afraid some of your old construction buddies will put two and two together. You're a coward.

HANDSOME: How dare you! Stand there in your greasy bathrobe and call me a coward. Do you know, do you even know what they would do to you, if they caught you?

MAXINE: What did they do?

HANDSOME: Chemical castration. A cocktail of some uncut poison that made damn sure you could never get it up again.

MAXINE: Did that—happen to you?

HANDSOME: I made damn sure it didn't.

MAXINE: Did it happen to him—

HANDSOME: I don't know for sure, but I think so.

MAXINE: Jesus.

HANDSOME: Ten years of the prime of his life. The career he loved, his friends, his home, his peace, his dignity … even the relationship to his own body. They used him … to scare the rest of us. We were hounded off the streets, out of our jobs, tossed in jail, beaten black and blue, and used for a goddamn Kleenex. [*pause*] After all that, say you manage to create some kind of a life. Find a bit of happiness, a bit of pleasure. Then a goddamn disease comes through like a merciless wolf …

MAXINE: I understand …

HANDSOME: [*with ferocity*] No you don't. You read about it, but you didn't live it.

MAXINE: You're right.

HANDSOME: And now you want me to be what? A role model for you? Why should I if the first time you hit a bump in the road you sit down and cry.

MAXINE: A bump in the road? You, you have no idea.

HANDSOME: Tell me then. What's so bad?

MAXINE: My girlfriend cheated on me.

I messed up at work.

HANDSOME: Oh boo hoo. Aren't you the country song. Did your truck break down too? Did the dog run away?

MAXINE: And this project, I mean no one will want to publish it if the public thinks Klippert is a pedophile.

HANDSOME: [*he holds himself in pain*] Ah …

[*EVERETT, too. On his bunk he holds his own side as if suppressing a deep pain. As if the word itself could burn a hole in his guts.*]

MAXINE: Handsome, are you alright?

HANDSOME: See there it is. That is the word that hurts. Nothing else compares. Let me tell you Everett was no pedophile. Was he older than me? Yes. The guys around town, we all knew he was a softie. You could count on him at the end of the night for a few bucks or a warm meal. But he never hurt anyone, never forced anyone. We took advantage of *him*, for god's sakes. You have to understand it wasn't like it is now, it was …

MAXINE: A different day.

HANDSOME: Yes. And we were all so ashamed that we couldn't help one another. I wanted to. When my father contacted the police—

MAXINE: Your father? Was your father the one who reported Klippert?

HANDSOME: [*these words cost him dearly*] Yes. And if you … knew how many times I wished I could go back in time and fight for him. But we couldn't fight for one another. We were too busy fighting ourselves.

MAXINE: Oh …

HANDSOME: And the idea of having a life together, sharing a home … wasn't imaginable for us. Maybe for your generation. But no, now your girlfriend took a little roll in the hay because you weren't letting her into the honey pot, so you're ready to throw in the towel.

MAXINE: How can I trust her now.

HANDSOME: Let's talk about trust. Does she know you don't talk to your father?

MAXINE: I can't—

HANDSOME: Does he know that you love him, that you want him in your life? Have you even told him?

MAXINE: Stop it.

HANDSOME: Does your lover know what a little timid mouse you are, deep in your soul.

MAXINE: Stop that.

HANDSOME: Do you love her?

MAXINE: YES!

HANDSOME: Is there nothing on this earth you are willing to fight for? Not your family, not Everett, not even your own lover, you little mouse of a woman?

[*MAXINE leaps off the sofa, charges over, and yells into his face.*]

MAXINE: I AM NOT A MOUSE!

HANDSOME: Aha. There you are. There you are at last.

[*HANDSOME walks over to her. Puts a tender hand on her cheek.*]

Fight for her. If it matters, fight for one another.

[*Lights fade.*]

Scene 27
(*space suit*)

EVERETT: There is a mismatch between the world as I imagine it and the world that is there when I open my eyes. People are not often … kind to a fellow like me. So I have lived … another life inside my head, I suppose. While I was in jail, they would play the first moments of the moon landing over and over on the television.

[*We hear the faint sounds of the original broadcast in the background, undercut with some static.*]

I imagined I was out there with them. Neil Armstrong and Buzz Aldrin. I was all sealed up in a space suit … walking free. I could do that. Maybe I can do that too.

[*He speaks to the audience as if they were the board of appeals.*]

If you let me out of here, I will walk so slowly, so carefully. I will lock myself in a space suit. Just like Neil and Buzz. I won't ever touch anyone ever again.

[*EVERETT gently speaks along with the broadcast:*]

"That's one small step for man; one giant leap for mankind … "

Scene 28
(*I bet he ate there*)

TONYA and MAXINE arrive at Handsome's room at the senior's complex. This is the first time they have seen each other in some time and awkwardness hangs in the air.

TONYA: Hi.

MAXINE: Hi.

TONYA: [*looking around*] Whoa you're right this place really is swank.

MAXINE: I know, right?

[*Beat.*]

TONYA: Max. I was so glad to get your message. I've been climbing the walls—

MAXINE: I needed time.

TONYA: Ah … man, is this a "here's your last shoe box of stuff" kind of a meeting? 'Cause if it is, just pull off the band aid, okay? I can't—

MAXINE: No. It's not.

[*TONYA lets out her breath.*]

TONYA: Okay. I mean if it is … this is a weird place to do it. [*beat*] I know I fucked up. And it's so complicated right. It's not just the sex, it's the breach of trust, it does damage. Damage that might not even be fixable and I know I should have talked to—

MAXINE: You tried; I wasn't listening.

TONYA: Instead of running off for some attention from a clearly intoxicated bouncer … if it makes you feel better she wasn't any good.

[*Silence.*]

Too soon? Too soon. What I mean to say … What I mean to say is I am just … [*puts her hands on Maxine's shoulder, looks in her eyes*] Looking you in the eye and I am … Sorry. I *am* sorry. That has to count for something, right?

MAXINE: Tonya.

TONYA: What?

MAXINE: It's me. It's me too. I compartmentalize … try to control outcomes … turn every bump in the road into some insurmountable …

[*Grabs Tonya in a hug.*]

TONYA: Come here.

[*After a moment, the embrace loosens and they look around.*]

Seriously this place is the Ritz! I would check in here right now if I could afford it.

MAXINE: Me too. Wonder if they have double suites…

TONYA: Is that a wet bar back there?

MAXINE: Shh!

TONYA: You two just sit in here, tell dirty stories, and get blasted every Tuesday, don't you? If that's what you call work, sign me up. Where's Handsome? I'm eager to meet your mystery man.

[*They look around.*]

MAXINE: We're a couple minutes early he's probably in a class or something.

[*After a moment.*]

TONYA: Really. Wow, okay … So what happened at work?

MAXINE: I explained somewhat and ah … they are going to give me another shot.

TONYA: How did you explain your absence…

MAXINE: I finally got the nerve to go see the Dean. There was this awful pause … And the pause kind of filled in with all kinds of horrible potentials … Suddenly I just channelled you.

TONYA: Me?

MAXINE: Yes, I said: "Everyone screws up sometimes." I said: "This was mine. Can I get a do-over?"

TONYA: What did he say.

MAXINE: I think he was totally relieved. Tapped a stack of papers on the edge of his desk, and said "Great. We'll let you get back to work and revisit this in a month's time."

TONYA: That's great.

MAXINE: Who knew human communication could be this straight-forward. And on that note … I have to tell you something. I know I have to change. I have to listen, really listen. That is if we are still—

TONYA: We are still! I mean if you want—

MAXINE: I still want, I still very much want.

TONYA: Oh good.

[*They grab hands and squeeze for a moment.*]

I brought this for lunch.

[*TONYA pulls some boxes from Chicken on the Way.*]

MAXINE: Chicken on the Way!

TONYA: You think he'll like it?

[*EVERETT gets up from his bunk, walks behind them, and grabs a chicken leg and eats it.*]

MAXINE: I think he will.

TONYA: I bet he ate there himself, back in the day.

MAXINE: Place hasn't changed since the sixties.

TONYA: Maybe he picked up his dinners from that same melamine counter.

MAXINE: He did—and picked up his dates there too. Handsome will love that.

TONYA: [*looking around*] Where is he by the way. I'll go ask at the desk.

[*A pause. MAXINE looks around the room. Some things are in boxes. TONYA comes back in with the knowledge that Handsome has passed visible on her face.*]

MAXINE: No …

TONYA: Sunday evening. The staff tried to get in touch.

MAXINE: But he was doing better. Why now?

[*TONYA puts her arm around Maxine.*]

TONYA: There's going to be service. We'll go together. Come here. It's okay.

MAXINE: It's not okay.

TONYA: It'll be okay.

MAXINE: I wanted you to meet him.

TONYA: I feel like I did. Through you, I did.

[*TONYA holds her. Behind the two of them, HANDSOME enters. He is his younger self, beautiful, confident. He sees EVERETT, goes over to him, and embraces him.*]

Scene 29
(*if things had been different*)

EVERETT and HANDSOME stand in an otherworldly light at a bus stop.

HANDSOME: There's been a pardon.

EVERETT: Pardon me?

HANDSOME: I said there's been an apology and a formal—oh. Still a smile on your face.

EVERETT: You're better off smiling, come what may.

HANDSOME: After all they did to you. I've thought of you so often over the years.

EVERETT: I've thought of you too.

HANDSOME: You were right, all those years ago … The world has caught up with you now and no one has to run or hide or be ashamed. And the way they treated you all those years ago. They were wrong. You weren't sick.

EVERETT: Never was sick a day in my life.

[*HANDSOME hands him a folded bill.*]

What's this now.

HANDSOME: Here's the dollar I owe you.

EVERETT: You did well for yourself.

HANDSOME: Built half this damn city.

EVERETT: I read about it. Proud of you.

HANDSOME: If things had been different.

EVERETT: If they had been.

[*They shake hands at first and then* HANDSOME *pulls Everett into an embrace. Light swirls around them like pieces of snow in a snow globe.*]

[*The two couples embrace as the lights cast the four bodies in silhouette. We hear, in a sound montage, the 1969 speech "there's no place for the state in the bedrooms of the nation" along with a cry of "make love, not war," then sounds of the moon landing broadcast, then a wash of cheering from a joyous pride march … finally fading to the bird song of a prairie spring day.*]

The End

II

Klippert Family Album

Everett (far right) in front of the
Bridgeland School in Calgary, Alberta.

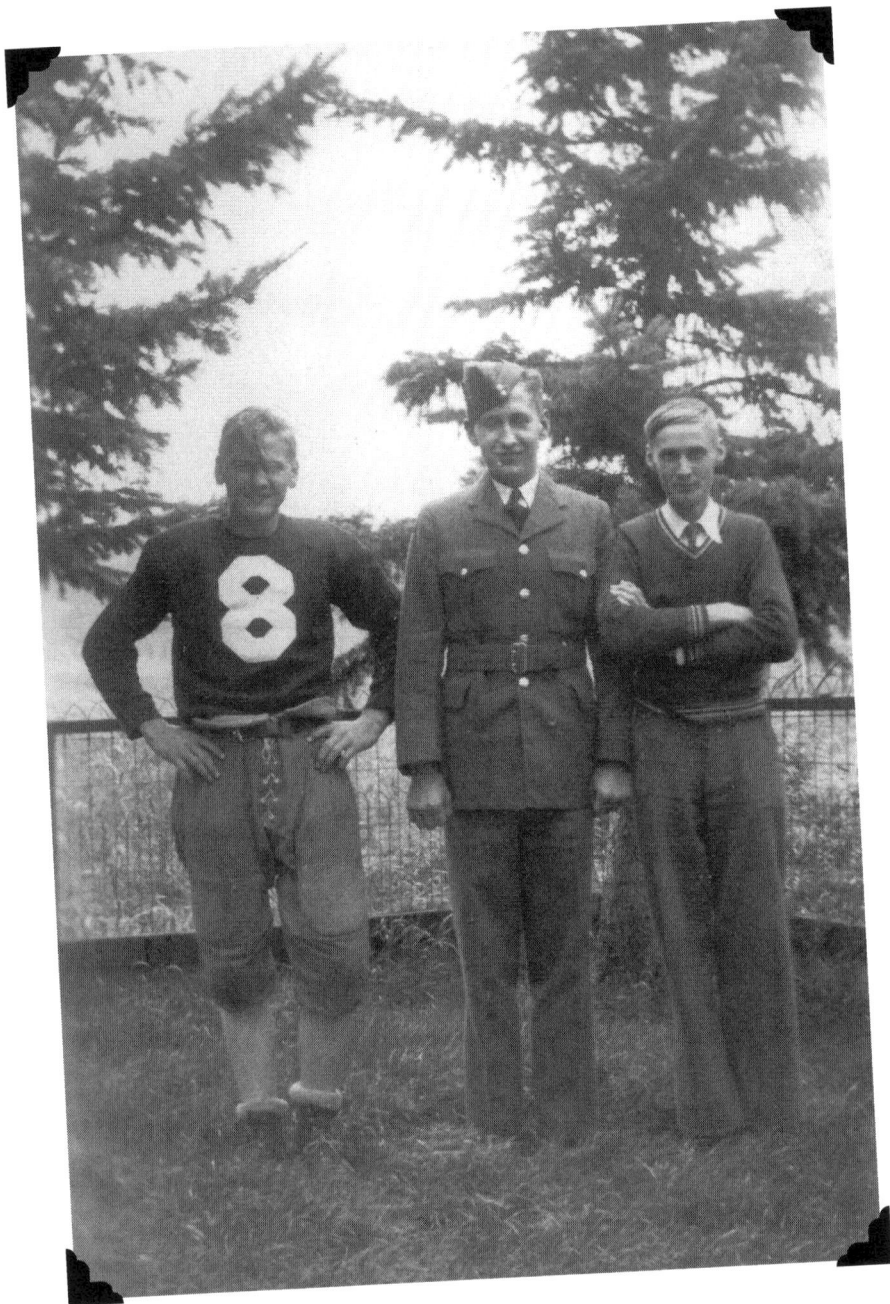

Everett Klippert (far right) poses for a photo with his brothers.

Everett Klippert (second from bottom right) at a family gathering.

Later in life Everett enjoyed peace and quiet,
and staying out of the public eye.

III

Bringing History to Life: Everett Klippert's Life and Times, and the Staging of *Legislating Love*

Our First Step towards Equality: The Life of Everett Klippert

Kevin Allen

Natalie Meisner's bursting-with-feeling play *Legislating Love* is based on a true story of profound injustice. In 1967 the Supreme Court of Canada upheld the 1965 Northwest Territories sentencing of Everett George Klippert—that he spend his life in prison just for being gay. The self-evident cruelty of the Supreme Court's decision would ultimately lead to the decriminalization of homosexuality in Canada.

While the public debate over Everett's legal case made him famous in Canada, many of the details of his life would not have been known without the support of his family. In addition to sharing their memories and insights into Everett's life, and allowing us to reproduce the family photos found in this book, they have also granted the Calgary Gay History Project permission to digitize and share this material online at https://calgarygayhistory.ca. Our thanks to the Klippert family for helping us preserve and share this important part of our history.

Everett was born in Kindersley, Saskatchewan in 1926, the youngest of nine siblings. His family relocated to Calgary when he was two years old. Initially renting a house on the city's North Hill, the Klipperts moved around frequently during their first few years in Calgary. Tragically, in May 1933, Everett's mother died from kidney disease.

In 1934, Everett's father bought a house in Crescent Heights, a bluff that overlooks the city's downtown. There, Everett's adult sister Leah took it upon herself to look after her eight younger brothers. The family was evangelical Baptist and Leah made sure that the family kept to its faith; they regularly attended services at the Crescent Heights Baptist Church.

School was not a priority for Everett, and he left after completing grade eight. Everett's father operated the Jenkin's grocery store in Bridgeland, and Everett's first job was working in the store along with some of his older brothers. His next job was working at Union Dairy; it was there that Everett had his first homosexual experiences at the age of sixteen or seventeen. After Union Dairy, he worked for eight years as a popular bus driver for Calgary Transit. A beloved personality, his regular passengers would skip earlier buses so that they could ride home with him due to his friendly, congenial nature.

In 1960, Everett came under police scrutiny. The father of a young man Everett had sex with learned of the affair between Everett and his son. Outraged, the father asked the police to investigate. On March 21, Everett was remanded into custody on a charge of "contributing to the delinquency of a young boy." His bail was set at $500.

On March 22, the very next day, his bail was increased to $9,000 as the crown brought more charges forward. Everett was charged with "indecent assault on 17 young Calgary boys" after to the discovery of his little black book, which documented his dating life. *The Albertan* newspaper (the predecessor of the *Calgary Sun*) wrote: "Klippert faced the court with bowed head Tuesday, elbows on the dock rail and face hidden in his hands, as the magistrate read the 17 new charges."

The unknown age of Everett's lovers, and their being termed "young boys" might cause consternation, but from what is known it is believed that Everett's sexual partners were young men, not children. In her essay "Through a Mirror Darkly: The Law and Society against Everett Klippert in Legislating Love," Tereasa Maillie covers this matter in greater detail, explaining how the charges against him imply that Everett's lovers were indeed adults. Douglas Elliott, a contemporary human rights lawyer who advocated to have a posthumous pardon issued for Everett and all men imprisoned for being gay in Canada, has also argued that because Everett's initial delinquency charge was withdrawn and substituted with a gross indecency one it likely meant the complainant was eighteen or that Everett honestly and reasonably believed him to be eighteen.

The trial was held on 2 and 4 May 1960, and Everett pled guilty. In speaking to sentencing, the Crown Prosecutor Ed Adolphe put forward evidence that Everett frequented boxing matches, wrestling matches, swimming pools, and other places where he was likely to come in contact with young men. Adolphe further alleged that as a bus driver Everett allowed them to ride free of charge, gaining their friendship.

Klippert's defence lawyer, Derek Maguire, told the court that Everett had a psychiatric assessment, which proposed that his homosexual tendencies arose from an unhappy childhood, given that his mother died when he was five years old. Maguire asked Justice Hugh Farthing to consider placing Everett on probation.

During sentencing, Justice Farthing described the case as "a particularly painful and distressing matter." He cited the UK's Wolfenden Report, which recommended homosexual behaviour between consenting adults in private should no longer be an offence. However, about Canada he added: "The law of the country, rightly or wrongly, regards this weakness as a crime, and my sworn duty is to administer the law of the country. We don't know what harm has been done to these boys . . . They were not developed and were easily influenced by a man older than themselves."

With that, Justice Farthing sentenced Everett to a four-year term in the Prince Albert Penitentiary for each of the eighteen charges. The sentences were to run concurrently, however, so Everett faced a total of four, and not seventy-two, years in prison. The judge also advised the court of his temperance in sentencing: the maximum penalty he could have given was five years for each charge, and if served consecutively that would have meant life imprisonment for Everett.

Upon his release in 1964, Everett tried to resume a normal life in Calgary. He moved in with one of his brothers and became engaged to a family friend named Betty Tutt. However, he feared that his continued presence in Calgary was bringing shame to his family, so in secret he interviewed with a local agent for a job as a mechanic's helper in the Northwest Territories. Everett got the job and moved to Pine Point the day before his wedding, jilting Betty in the process.

Everett proved popular at Pine Point. In an interview with the Calgary Gay History Project, Bob Johnson, who was Everett's boss at Pine Point, said that, "everybody loved him—he was such a damn nice guy." Everett was one of the few men who had a car. On days off, Everett would regularly gather up a bunch of guys and drive everyone to Hay

River, forty miles down the road, where they would go to the movies or go drinking.

Despite his good reputation, the local RCMP knew of Everett's past convictions, and kept an eye on him. Using a round-up of possible suspects in a Pine Point arson case as an excuse, on 15 August 1965 the RCMP brought in Everett for questioning. The RCMP quizzed him about his criminal file and homosexuality. According to Everett, he was told that unless he pleaded guilty to homosexuality he would be charged with arson. Consequently, Everett admitted to having had consensual homosexual sex with four different men in the Northwest Territories. He was subsequently arrested, charged with four counts of gross indecency, and sentenced to three more years in prison. Three months into his prison sentence, he was given official notice that the Crown was petitioning to have him declared "a dangerous sexual offender." A court-ordered psychiatrist assessed the mild-mannered Everett as an "incurable homosexual," and he was sentenced to "preventive detention," indefinitely, just for being gay.

Everett was not alone in his struggle. His older sister Leah Klippert, who worked as a legal secretary in the offices of J. D. Salmon, solicitor for the city of Calgary, dedicated herself to seeking justice for her brother. She wrote Everett's legal correspondence, engaged lawyers on his behalf, and appealed his court verdicts as unjust. Ultimately, her efforts pushed his case to the Supreme Court of Canada, but the appeal at the Supreme Court was dismissed in a controversial 3–2 decision on 7 November 1967.

Leah's efforts also pushed Everett's case into the court of public opinion, and his case began to gain notoriety as it moved through the legal system and to the Supreme Court. After the Supreme Court's decision, the *Globe and Mail* declared that, "It is strange to the point of being unbelievable that conduct in Britain, which would not even bring a criminal charge, can, in Canada, send a man to prison for life." The *Winnipeg Free Press* editorialized: "It is possible to deplore such activity without treating its practitioners as if they were monsters." Even *The Albertan*, a newspaper that typically opposed gay liberation, wrote: "the spectre of a possible life sentence seems to us a little severe." The only metropolitan newspaper in Canada that seems to have reacted in support of the decision by the Supreme Court was the *Edmonton Journal*, which opposed homosexual law reform because of the purported tendency of homosexuals to prey on the young.

The waves Everett's case made cascaded through the news media and to the House of Commons. The Supreme Court decision prompted then Minister of Justice Pierre Elliott Trudeau's famous quote, delivered to a media scrum outside the House of Commons on 21 December 1967: "Take this thing on homosexuality, I think the view we take here is that there's no place for the state in the bedrooms of the nation, and I think what's done in private between adults doesn't concern the Criminal Code."

A few months later, in April of 1968, Trudeau became Prime Minister of Canada. His Minister of Justice John Turner presented the Criminal Law Amendment Act (Bill C-150). It became law in 1969, and, among other things, decriminalized homosexual acts between consenting male adults.

Throughout the process of decriminalizing homosexuality, police from across the country were opposed to the change. For example, in 1967 when Everett's case was in the news, Calgary Police Chief Ken McIver reportedly declared that the new law represented the decay of Canadian society. The *Toronto Star* quoted McIver as saying that homosexuality is "a horrible, vicious, and terrible thing." Indeed, he added, "we do not need it in this country."

Despite making national news, and despite his case acting as the catalyst for the decriminalization of homosexuality in Canada, Everett inexplicably remained in prison until 21 July 1971 (Tereasa Maillie explores this further in her essay). Upon release from prison, Everett left the spotlight. For the remainder of his life Everett kept a low profile, even adopting his middle name, George, as a new first name. He later married a great friend of his, Dorothy Hagstrom, and lived a quiet life until he died of kidney disease in 1996.

In 2018, Everett's story made a posthumous return to Calgary. In March, Sage Theatre's production of Natalie Meisner's play, *Legislating Love: The Everett Klippert Story* premiered to great acclaim. A few months later, in July, the Calgary Police Service formally apologized to Calgary's gender and sexually diverse community. In their official statement, they cited their historic opposition to Bill C-150 and said: "after the law changed our organization struggled to embrace the new direction and evolve."

Thanks to one unassuming Calgary bus driver, the trajectory of LGBTQ2 rights in Canada changed with Bill C-150. Thanks to Everett, we took our first step towards equality.

Through a Mirror Darkly: The Law and Society against Everett Klippert in *Legislating Love*

Tereasa Maillie

Legislating Love follows the journey of Calgary bus driver Everett George Klippert, whose life was not only deeply affected by Canadian law, but whose life also ultimately challenged and changed Canadian law. Through Klippert, the play's audience is shown a dark part of Canada's past when homosexuality[1] was illegal. Due to the natural constrictions of playwriting, *Legislating Love* could not delve into the intricate historical backstory of Calgary and the legalization of homosexuality. In the audience talk-back sessions held during the readings and production of the play, the audience had a chance to ask the creators and historians more about this era that Klippert lived in—what was life like for homosexuals in Calgary, how the laws regarding homosexuality change because of his legal case, and so on. This essay expands on those talk-back sessions and aims to give more fulsome answers to these and other questions.

Klippert passed away in 1996, so unfortunately he is no longer here to tell his own story—what life was like for him, and how his part in the decriminalization of homosexuality affected him. Even within the personal papers that the Klippert family gifted to the *Legislating Love* playwrights and historians there is no direct mention of Everett's feelings or memories of the 1950s and 1960s. However, we can utilize many other personal histories from queer community members, as well as oral history interviews, newspaper reports, and court documents, to compile an image of how society and the law treated homosexual men at that time.

In pre-1969 Canada, the overwhelming attitude toward homosexuals was one of ignorance, fear, and disgust, and it was only when society changed (due in part to Klippert's case) that the laws changed as well. In its depictions of the covert and dangerous relationship Klippert had with the character of the closeted gay man Handsome, as well as Klippert's two arrests, *Legislating Love* shows how this time in Calgary was a time of oppression. Calgary's shift in the late 1960s to a limited acceptance of homosexuality was interwoven with rhetoric on mental illness and damnation. Nevertheless, homosexuals possessed a level of agency and self-determination—evident in the creation, despite social and legal challenges, of their own community's safe spaces.

The 1950s and 1960s laws in Canada were based on old English laws, which held that gay men were "perverts." These ideas were still being firmly upheld by police and the courts when Klippert was arrested in 1960 and 1967. With the advocacy of the public, Everett's family, and his lawyer, the government was finally able to see that a change was needed. An amendment to the criminal code decriminalizing homosexuality was passed in 1969, but the protection it afforded to homosexuals was limited. Even though it was Klippert's case that ignited change, Everett himself remained in prison until 1971. This is the dark mirror that historians, playwright Natalie Meisner, and other interested members of the public have tried to look into—but very few answers have been found. Why Klippert remained in prison almost two years after decriminalization is still difficult to understand.

Klippert's Calgary

The first scene in *Legislating Love* shows Everett Klippert working as a bus driver in 1960s Calgary. His bus would have travelled through a fast-moving and growing sprawl. The city's population had grown from 104,718 people in 1950 to double that size by 1960.[2] Normative quotidian life was centred around the ideal nuclear family, a middle-class lifestyle with marriage and children.[3] In regards to gender and sexuality diversity, Calgarian culture was based on a heteronormative narrative of working fathers and homemaker mothers. Historian Bryan Palmer believed that this was part of the postwar project of rebuilding society and the economy: "People were searching for security and relative prosperity, resulting in a strengthening of patriarchal authority and privilege for men in heterosexual circumstances."[4]

Homosexuals like Klippert were not included in Calgary's public narrative. For example, in a literature review I conducted, the terms *gay men*, *homosexual*, and *lesbian* did not appear in any issues of *The Albertan* newspaper in two years that we know Klippert lived in Calgary: 1950 and 1959. Upon first reading one is given the impression that no homosexuals existed in Calgary. The image the city portrayed to the outside world and to itself was straight, as evident in the 1962 promotional video "The Living West." Part tourist promotion and part narrative of white superiority, the film shows a family visiting the hometown of the dad; the wife is well dressed and the kid is happy and loves to eat Alberta beef.[5] The video was an attempt to envision Calgary as a modern and exciting destination for families, and men like Klippert were not a part of this vision of Calgary. It reinforces the invisibility of homosexuals in the media and the bias of the times to ignore anything outside heteronormativity. This exclusion continues through to the modern era. In a review of twenty books on Calgary's history, published from 1950 to 2000 and held at the Calgary Public Library, none of them mention any queer people or communities. Despite the omission of homosexuals from Calgary's history, the seeds of a future queer community existed from the time of the first settlers. In *Prairie Fairies: A History of Queer Communities and People in Western Canada, 1930–1985*, historian Valerie Korinek rightly asserts that many queer urban and rural people lived and loved in the prairies, but that their history has been marginalized or omitted from Canada's historical story.[6] Many of the seniors she interviewed point out that a community did not exist as it does today—many chose to keep a low profile, and with good reason. Calgary's Dr. Carolyn Anderson wrote in her thesis "The Voices of Older Lesbian Women: An Oral History" that as a social worker in the 1960s and 1970s she had to keep her personal life and work life separate: "I feared the rejection of my ideas, loss of status, loss of my previous safe identity in the professional fields, and that doors to future jobs would close."[7]

Oral interviews with Elsie McRobbie—a long-time Calgary resident, social activist, and my maternal aunt—support this perspective. McRobbie asserted in an interview in 2015 that many homosexual men and women were her friends as a teen in 1950s. She had a strong sense of protectiveness toward the gay men she had known since she was a child:

> No one I knew was openly fairy, or gay. They were very quiet about it—I had a few friends in high school and they would never use the words, but we knew, 'cause they'd hang out with us. But they were scared if anyone found out they'd get beaten up. Your grandma's cousin A. was like our dad to us, but a "confirmed bachelor," right? So my mom told me one day he liked to be with men only. She said to me that there was nothing wrong about it really, God loved everyone, we needed to never say anything though; we had to protect him because they'd take him away, the police.[8]

Echoing McRobbie's attitudes, queer activist Lois Szabo remembered the pressure on women to remain hidden from their families. In an interview with CBC, she said life in Calgary in the 1950s and 1960s pushed many heterosexual norms for women: "You went to school, got married and had children." Szabo herself married and had children, and while her husband was kind and understanding when she came out to him, she recalled that a couple across the street was the exact opposite. When that wife "came out" to her husband as a lesbian he had her committed to a hospital for six weeks. She came home "promising not to go that route again" but when she did, "he took the children away to Quebec."[9]

The institutionalization of that woman represents part of a larger discourse in Canadian and Calgarian society: that homosexuality was a mental disorder. Albertans and physicians in general at the time viewed homosexuality as a personality disturbance that should be treated. Treatment plans pre-1969 from Alberta's psychiatric treatment centres such as the Ponoka Institute are not declassified, but generalized approaches from medical journal do provide some insights.[10] From North American medical journals we have some ideas on approaches to treatment, including using anticipatory avoidance learning, conditioning, and psychotherapy.[11] A list of common treatments in 1968 includes the use of hormones, shocking the patient with the drug metrazol, carbon dioxide inhalations, electric aversion conditioning, and chemical aversion therapy using apomorphone.[12] How familiar homosexuals in Alberta were with the details of various treatments is not known, but most were fully aware of the possibilities of being institutionalized. Carol Anderson interviewed one woman, Donna, who worked in the "helping profession" in the 1960s who said she never discussed being a lesbian: "I was very quiet about it when I was in training. They would have made me take my uniform off and put me in one of the padded cells, you know. Yeah I was really cautious at that time."[13]

While many people believed homosexuality was a mental illness, many believed it was also a sin. In 1961, there were 18.24 million people in Canada, 97 per cent of whom were Christians.[14] No Christian religion at this time was supportive of homosexuality; it was considered a sin. This did not mean that it should be ignored, but that the churches had a duty to minister to homosexuals. Pierre Berton, in his 1965 text *The Comfortable Pew: A Critical Look at Christianity and the Religious Establishment in the New Age*, was critical of the Christian clergy ignoring the needs of homosexuals and treating them as lepers.[15] That same year, Reverend Richard E. Clark of the Anglican Church of the Holy Trinity in Calgary spoke out in support of Berton's opinion that the churches had overlooked the problem of homosexuality and were letting psychiatrists and government deal with it instead. Clark stated that while homosexuality was sinful, it was no worse than other sins: "If the Anglican Church of Canada wishes to make a significant contribution to the work of God then let us announce without hedging we invite you, the homosexuals and lesbians, into our pews."[16]

If homosexuals like Everett Klippert were somehow viewed as simultaneously non-existent, breaking the law, mentally ill, and sinners that needed to be saved, then where could they find safety in Calgary? Private parties, as well as hotel bars that would allow them, were the two kinds of spaces most cited by elders in oral interviews.[17] Elsie McRobbie recalled in the late 1950s as a teenager going to one of these private parties in an apartment: "a lesbian I knew [warned me] that there'd be only queer guys there so I wouldn't get any dates."[18] Many homosexuals did venture to bars that tolerated their patronage: women predominantly went to the Cecil Hotel bar on 4th Avenue SE. Men went to socialize at the Carlton Hotel on 9th Avenue sw, the Red Fox at the Empire Hotel, or Kings Arms Tavern inside the Palliser Hotel. Called "the Pit," the Kings Arms was a well-known and popular spot since the 1930s and was still in operation until the 1970s, serving straight men in the front and homosexuals in the back rooms.[19] Nick de Vos, who was active in the creation of a visible gay community, recalled the times at the Kings Arms Tavern:

> Most of us had to enter through the front entrance and worked our way to the bar as the First Street bar entrance was too obvious—there was a danger of getting known and losing your job. When the bar closed everyone placed $1.00 on the table for someone to buy beer to keep the party going at someone's apartment. There was always a volunteer host for those parties which went into the wee hours of the morning on weekends.[20]

However, the King's Arms was run by a straight man. Where were the clubs that were run by and for homosexuals? This would change with the opening of the 620 Club, renamed later to the 1207 Club as it moved to a new address. It began as a club for anyone, but in 1967 the club's owner decided to operate it as a "gay club" and sold tickets to straight people to come down to "look at the queers." The 1207 Club was boycotted by gay people, according to Lois Szabo, and from its ashes she and her friends created the first club for their community—Club Carousel.[21] Taken over by the gay- and lesbian-run Scarth Street Society, they opened their club in the spring of 1968. By creating their own clubs exclusively for themselves, the first active gay community organization in Calgary was established. It was a much-needed safe haven: since Club Carousal operated as a private club that followed provincial charter legislations, a "no straights allowed" policy could be enforced. This creation and enforcement of their own safe spaces was for a serious reason.

Not only could they be arrested and placed in jail, risk being outed, and lose their jobs or families, queer people could also be verbally and physically assaulted. There is no data on physical violence against male homosexuals in the 1960s, but many interviewees mention getting roughed up by police and heterosexual men across the country from Vancouver to Montreal.[22]

Everett Klippert missed the beginnings of the active gay community in Calgary: instead he was imprisoned twice, and become an unlikely beacon for the decriminalization of homosexuality in Canada. However Klippert himself was held in prison until 1971. To explain why this happened to Klippert, we have to go back to the origins of our criminal code.

Canada's legal system is based on the English and French systems of law that colonists brought to Canada in the seventeenth and eighteenth centuries. In Britain homosexuality had been outlawed in the Buggery Act of 1533, which was the first legal instance of male homosexuality being targeted for persecution in the UK.[23] The Buggery Act completely outlawed sodomy and bestiality in Britain, and by extension across the entire British Empire. All convictions were punishable by death. Instead of softening the original laws, the British Criminal Law Amendment Act in 1885 made any male homosexual act illegal.[24] From this, Canada developed its own legal approach to male homosexuality. The first Canadian Criminal Code in 1892 placed homosexuality under two sections: "Acts of gross indecency "and "Indecent assaults on males." Both were concerned with anal sex between men, and both were punishable by whipping and liable to five to seven years' imprisonment. The 1940 criminal code, in article XIII, "Offences against Morality," states that both bestiality and buggery had the same punishment: "Every one is guilty of an indictable offence and liable to imprisonment for life who commits buggery, either with a human being or with any other living creature ... Every one is guilty of an indictable offence and liable to ten years' imprisonment who attempts to commit the offence mentioned."[25]

In Alberta, these laws were used to actively prosecute male homosexuals. In reviewing the *Globe and Mail* newspaper from 1900 to 1965, there are no reports of women being arrested for same-sex relations or gross indecency. As the criminal code focused on buggery, men were the focus of sex crimes, with decision to prosecute depending on factors including if a complaint was lodged to the police, if there were witnesses, and if the police and other legal authorities wanted to pursue these cases.[26] In 1935 Alberta's election of the Social Credit government brought in Premier William "Bible Bill" Aberhart, a teacher and Baptist radio evangelist. Aberhart held firm to fundamentalist Christian principles that did not permit homosexuality; these Christian principles were heard in his many speeches and broadcasts, where God and good government are linked.[27] Premier Aberhart also assumed the office of Alberta's attorney general at this time. His correspondence with senior RCMP officers in 1942 suggests that the investigation of moral offences was a particular concern for him.[28] That year, the RCMP and Edmonton's municipal constabulary arrested ten men on charges of gross indecency and buggery.[29] The arrests and trials generated widespread publicity and a "moral panic" among the general public. Six men were found guilty and punished.[30] Just as in the play Klippert is forced to give up his little black book of personal information on various men, so too was the private correspondence of these men seized and used to secure confessions.

Almost twenty years later, in the 1960s, attitudes toward gay men seemed to have not shifted much either in Calgary or in Canada at large. In 1960, the *Globe and Mail* reported the murder of a homosexual man more as an unfortunate accident than as a crime. Joseph Normandin stabbed Alexander Balkis, a confirmed homosexual, to death after Balkis purportedly approached him for sex. "A class of man whose victims were generally boys . . . he (Balkis) had perverted many boys but in meeting Normandin, he had picked someone who was ill and abnormal."[31] The outcome was that the murder charge stood but the sentence was reduced in light of Balkis' "abnormality."

Klippert's Two Trials

Into this legal environment came Everett Klippert. His first arrest was 21 March 1960.[32] As retold in the play, the father of a "boy" Klippert had relations with complained to the police. Klippert was remanded into custody without a plea on a charge of contributing to the delinquency of a juvenile, and bail was set at $500. Things quickly worsened when Klippert was asked about his little black book, which was filled with names and addresses of men. Klippert admitted that he had been seeing and having relations with these men. As a result, on 23 March the Crown brought seventeen more charges forward. His name and address were printed in the local paper.[33] He was found guilty of indecent assault, which implies that the sexual contact was not wholly consensual; however, in April he instead pleaded guilty to eighteen counts of gross indecency, meaning that the sex was consensual but still illegal. He was sentenced to four years in prison.[34]

After being released, Klippert moved immediately to the mining community of Pine Point, Northwest Territories. But this attempt at a quieter life was not to be. While working at the mine as a mechanic's helper, Klippert continued to have same-sex relations. Suddenly on 16 August 1965 the RCMP detained him based on suspicion of arson against the mine manager's home. Why Klippert? We can assume that the local RCMP had been keeping tabs on Klippert, as his previous conviction for gross indecency would have alerted the investigators that he was a homosexual. This was also the era of paranoia and the RCMP hunt for homosexuals. As historian Gary Kinsman uncovered in his research, the RCMP had been targeting homosexuals for years in Ottawa and across Canada.[35] From the 1950s to the late 1990s, police and RCMP interrogated, harassed, and targeted homosexuals as they were viewed as threats to society and enemies of the state based on the false assumption that they were liable to be blackmailed by Soviet spies.[36] According to an interview with the arresting RCMP officer Corporal Jim Armstrong in 2002, Klippert was definitely targeted; as Armstrong said: "arsonists were deviants and homosexuals were deviants."[37]

Armstrong's comment is in line with the prevailing attitudes for centuries, and as mentioned earlier, homosexuality was lumped together with bestiality and child molestation under the criminal codes of Britain and Canada. Psychiatry agreed that any deviance from heterosexuality was abnormal. Called sexual inverts, homosexuals, and child molesters, "lower" humans such as prisoners and Black men were seen as animals, a sub-class of human, all deviant and dangerous.[38] Klippert's case is peppered with references to his "boys," implying that he was also a child molester.[39] No evidence exist in the court records that Klippert was a child molester and the exact ages of the men he was involved with are given as a range or omitted. But society and the law were vague on male consent. In 1960 there was no age of consent listed in the criminal code for same-sex relations, since the entire act was illegal. In the 1960s, the legal definition of a juvenile was more dependent on the case, and could be anyone from the ages of five to seventeen.[40] Additionally, the age of consent in the Canadian criminal code was not applied to boys or men, but focused on women/girls exclusively. From 1892 to 1988, there was no mention of age of consent for men (boys) when the legal age for women (girls) was listed as fourteen. This did not change until gay rights and child protection advocates demanded that the proposed Bill C-15 in 1988 address the age of consent for boys as well as anal sex, as it was illegal for any Canadian under the age of fifteen.[41] The law was amended and passed, making the age of consent seventeen and legalizing anal sex between consenting adults.

Klippert was never changed with arson, but he was charged with gross indecency with four different men. It is hard to discern what legal counsel he received, but Klippert pleaded guilty to all four charges of gross indecency and was sentenced to three years in prison. The four men specifically mentioned in the case that Klippert had sexual relations with were never charged.[42] The law was not finished with him: the crown prosecutor decided to push hard for a conviction under the dangerous offender laws. A conviction of buggery, indecent assault on a male, or gross indecency allowed for preventative detention, meaning that a habitual criminal who was deemed an ongoing danger to society could be held in prison indefinitely.[43] As required by law, two psychiatrists had to examine Klippert and provide evidence to the court that this designation was justified. Both psychiatrists testified that they viewed homosexuality as a mental illness, and that Klippert had confessed his homosexuality to them—but both psychiatrists also believed that Klippert was not violent. They did admit that he was likely to commit further sexual offences (same-sex relations) with other consenting adult males. This sealed it for the courts. Under the existing laws, along with his previous convictions in 1960, Klippert was deemed an ongoing danger to society and was to be placed in preventative detention for an indefinite period.

Klippert and his lawyer B. A. Crane appealed to the Supreme Court in November 1967. Supreme Court Judge Cartwright argued that the law invoked by parliament was never intended to lock up all homosexuals permanently, and that prison would be full to capacity if they tried. The testimony by the two psychiatrists was key as well. Both doctors had stated that Klippert had always been a homosexual, that the behaviour had existed since the age of fifteen, that he was ill and needed help, and that:

> he never had had heterosexual relations, that during twenty-four years of fairly active homosexual practice he had many partners whose ages varied from the middle teens to 30 or 35 . . . there was no suggestion whatsoever of any violence at any time; that he was most co-operative through the interview, restrained in manner, courteous, coherent, relevant and frank.[44]

Despite the psychiatrist recommendations, they did state that Klippert would not stop, in their opinion, and that he could not control his sexual impulses. Supreme Court Judge Hall argued that under the law, just like bestiality gross indecency could be a danger to society if the person was likely to commit future sexual offences. Based on this, the judges dismissed the appeal 3–2.

At the time no one knew the full weight and consequence of this failed appeal on Canadian society and law. The newspapers, including Calgary's daily *The Albertan*, called for Klippert's release as there was no evidence of him being violent or a danger to society. These newspapers cited the idea that homosexuality was a mental illness, not a criminal offence.[45] The full impact of the Klippert case also startled many, in that it set the dangerous precedent in Canadian law that any homosexual found guilty could potentially be imprisoned for life. Bud Orange, the Liberal MP for Northwest Territories, said that the law should be amended along the British pattern to permit relations between consenting adults: "It's absolutely ridiculous that any man in our society would be put in jail because he is affected by a social disease."[46] The legal and psychiatric communities also called for changes based on this high-profile case. Lawyer Alex Gigeroff, working for the Clarke Institute of Psychiatry, stated that the charge of gross indecency used to cover homosexuality and other sexual acts was too vague. He said that sexual acts between any two adults over the age of twenty-one was a question of personal morality rather than a legal question. Gigeroff also pointed out that buggery and bestiality should be separated in the code.[47] Interestingly, he does not mention the institute's position on homosexuality as a mental illness, but instead focuses on the notion that the law does not go far enough and should be removed, not amended.

Behind the headlines, Klippert sat in prison. We don't know what his thoughts were, but we do know that he had the support of two key people. His sister Leah was a staunch defender, and she had a background in law. She retained Calgary/Yukon lawyer William Wuttunee, the first Cree lawyer in western Canada.[48] The meeting of these two would change the pathway of decriminalization in Canada. While he and Leah kept the appeal alive, Wuttunee also contacted federal NDP leader Tommy Douglas, who he had worked with many times on Indian issues in Saskatchewan when Douglas was premier. According to Wuttunee's friend Penney Kome, Douglas then brought the case to the attention of then-justice minister Pierre Trudeau.[49] When Douglas questioned Trudeau in the House of Commons, Trudeau suggested the creation of a committee to look at the issue, and appointed Mr. Justice Robert Ouimet to head the study.[50] One key element for the study was that the British law had already changed in 1967. Based on the Wolfenden Report from 1957, Britain passed *The Sexual Offences Act*, which decriminalized homosexual acts taking place in private between two men both over the age of twenty-one.[51]

In 1969 Pierre Trudeau became prime minister, and pushed his justice minister John Turner to amend the criminal code. Trudeau's famous line "The state has no place in the bedrooms of the nation" was given in direct reference to the amendment and Klippert's case. The debate in the House of Commons was fierce: Turner pointed out that the criminal code was actually unchanged on gross obscenity, bestiality, and buggery. This was an amendment where individual relationships and areas of private conscience and private behaviour were better left to private judgement, he stated.[52] Opponents such as Progressive Conservative MP Walter Dinsdale argued that the prime minister's comment that the state has no place in the bedrooms of the nation was nonsense, that if a man committed a murder in a bedroom the state would move in, and that homosexuality was "a form of murder of the spirit."[53]

By 14 May 1969, the debate on Bill C-150 to amend the criminal code had carried. Buggery and indecent acts were still listed in the criminal code, but with the addendum that acts in private between husband and wife, or consenting adults over the age of twenty-one, were now legal.

The changes came into effect later that year (26 August), and were up-dated in the 1970 criminal code.[54] The floodgates of acceptance did not open, however—not even in the press. One month after Bill C-150 was passed, many publishers refused to run an article on Paul Bedard's fight for the rights of homosexuals in Canada; these recalcitrant publishers ripped the article out of the magazine *Weekend*, which was in syndica-tion in thirty-nine newspapers across Canada.[55]

A Mirror, Darkly

In *Legislating Love*, there is a scene that encapsulates the mystery of Everett Klippert's incarceration until 1971, as well as his own reflections on his case. Klippert looks into a mirror at the same time as Max, the historian looking into his life. Neither of them can see clearly, but both have a feeling of some great change and movement. The darkness for Max is more than just an image on stage. Historians and legal minds still do not understand fully why Everett was kept in prison for another two years (he was held at the Prince Albert Maximum Security Penitentiary.) One argument for why he was still in prison was that because Klippert lacked legal counsel he did not realize that he could continue to apply for release after the passage of Bill C-150.[56] This is not plausible, how-ever: Klippert had been involved in his appeals, had ongoing help from his legally informed sister Leah, and also had Mr. Wuttunee's continued assistance. The answer might be as mundane as that it took until 1971 for the courts to hear Klippert's case. A stronger argument is that the new law was not retroactive. Citing a Justice Department official's comments on the case, a 1969 *Montreal Gazette* article pointed out the irony of Klippert still sitting in jail as the amendment he helped to bring about was not being applied to his or any previous cases, and Klippert would have to remain in prison unless another legal challenge was mounted.[57] Details of how Klippert was eventually freed, and of Wuttunee's impact, are unclear and need to be studied further.

One might expect that Klippert would have become an activist after his legal challenges, but the complete opposite was true. After his release he lived a quiet life. He did not return to Calgary but instead moved to Edmonton, working as a truck driver but staying close to family. When he retired in the mid-1980s he married Dorothy Hagstrom. Klippert died of kidney disease in 1996. His nephew, Donald Klippert, cannot understand why his uncle was in prison so long: "Everett as a dangerous sexual offender is patently ridiculous. You couldn't ask for a nicer, more gentle person. He wouldn't harm a fly."[58] Klippert himself was tight-lipped about this period in his life, even with family, but he did keep a journal while he was in jail. The Klippert family has loaned Everett's personal documents to the Calgary Gay History project and to play-wright Natalie Meisner in the hopes of uncovering more about his cases. In examining his journals, what has emerged is an image of a man who kept busy in jail, reading Confucius and Rudyard Kipling. His own importance in the decriminalization of homosexuality is subtly realized in one short, poignant entry—some indication that he understood his impact in history: "August 26th 1969 Tuesday, the criminal code came into effect, due to my case."[59]

Notes

1 This essay will use the term "homosexuality," as it was the umbrella designation for same-sex relations socially, medically, and legally until the 1980s. When speaking on modern ideas on same-sex relations, other terms such as gay and queer will be used. Interestingly the term "queer" was a derogatory term in Klippert's lifetime but has been reclaimed and is now in daily use. For more details see Qmunity BC Queer Resource Centre, *Queer Terminology from A to Q*, 2013, https://qmunity.ca/resources/queer-glossary/

2 City of Calgary, "Municipal Manual," 1950, 1960.

3 James Onusko, "Suburbia and Community Development: What Were the Effects in 1950s Calgary?" (Master's thesis, Athabasca University, 2008), 24–5.

4 Bryan Palmer, *Canada's 1960s: The Ironies of Identity in a Rebellious Era* (Toronto: University of Toronto Press, 2009), 57.

5 Author unknown, "Calgary, The Living West (Film)" Calgary Convention and Visitor's Bureau, 1962, https://www.youtube.com/watch?v=DHpZcImE7Hs.

6 Valerie J. Korinek, *Prairie Fairies: A History of Queer Communities and People in Western Canada, 1930–1985* (Toronto: University of Toronto Press, 2018.)

7 Carolyn Anderson, *The Voices of Older Lesbian Women: An Oral History* (PhD thesis: University of Calgary, 2001), 4.

8 Elsie McRobbie (née Parker), interviewed by Tereasa Maillie, June 2015. McRobbie is the interviewer's maternal aunt.

9 Lois Szabo, unknown reporter, CBC Calgary, 25 Aug 2017. https://www.cbc.ca/news/canada/calgary/watch-lois-szabo-tell-her-story-of-coming-out-in-1960s-calgary-1.4263165.

10 Files released for research are accounting, business, and supply orders, with some patient ledgers with names and dates, but no diagnosis or treatment details. The majority of files are still under Freedom of information acts at the Provincial Archives of Alberta.

11 M. J. MacCulloch, C. J. Birtles, M. P. Feldman, "Anticipatory Avoidance Learning for the Treatment of Homosexuality: Recent Developments and an Automatic Aversion Therapy System," *Behavior Therapy* 2, no. 2 (April 1971): 151–69.

12 Tom Kraft, "A Case of Homosexuality Treated by Systematic Desensitization," *Journal of Psychotherapy* 21, no. 4 (1967): 815–21.

13 Anderson, *The Voices of Older Lesbian Women*, 118.

14 Statistics Canada, Table 17-10-0073-01: Historical statistics, principal religious denominations of the population, https://www150.statcan.gc.ca/t1/tbl1/en/ tv.action?pid=1710007301.

15 Pierre Berton, *The Comfortable Pew: A Critical Look at Christianity and the Religious Establishment in the New Age* (Toronto: McClelland and Stewart, 1965), 92–3, 112.

16 "City Cleric Claims Church Ignoring Homosexuality," *Calgary Herald*, 29 Mar 1965.

17 For lesbians, many also joined softball leagues in the city, however, there's no evidence that gay men saw this as a place of community.

18 Elsie McRobbie (née Parker), interviewed by Tereasa Maillie, June 2015.

19 Kevin Allen, *Our Past Matters: Stories of Gay Calgary* (Calgary: ASPublishing, 2018), 16.

20 Kevin Allen, "The Passing of Nick de Vos," *Calgary Gay History*, 24 Nov 2016. https://calgarygayhistory.ca/2016/11/24/the-passing-of-nick-de-vos/.

21 Kevin Allen, *Our Past Matters*, 36–9.

22 Tom Warner, *Never Going Back: A History of Queer Activism in Canada* (Toronto: University of Toronto Press, Scholarly Publishing Division, 2002), 38–9.

23 "Anno. XXV. Henrici VIII. Actis made in the session of this present parliament holden uppon prorogation at Westmynster, the .XV. daye of Januarie, in the. XXV. yere of the reigne of our moste dradde soueraygne lorde kynge Henry the. VIII. […] 1535." British Library. https://www.bl.uk/collection-items/ the-buggery-act-1533.

24 Steven Dryden, "A Short History of LGBT Rights in the UK," British Library LGTBQ Histories, https://www.bl.uk/lgbtq-histories/articles/a-short-history-of- lgbt-rights-in-the-uk.

25 1940 Canadian Criminal Code, R.S.C. 1927, c. 36. Part V Offences against Religion Morals and Public Convenience. http://www.constancebackhouse.ca/fileadmin/ website/1940.htm.

26 Lyle Dick, "The 1942 Same-Sex Trials in Edmonton: On the State's Repression of Sexual Minorities, Archives, and Human Rights in Canada," *Archivaria* 68 (2009): 188.

27 Fred Kennedy, Transcripts of William Aberhart's radio broadcasts, 1935. Glenbow Archives Fonds M-1621-(4-7). Transcripts of Sunday morning radio broadcasts, made from the Calgary Prophetic Bible Institute.

28 Dick, "The 1942 Same-Sex Trials in Edmonton," 193.

29 "26 Cases Listed in Supreme Court," *Edmonton Journal* (18 September 1942): 10.

30 Dick, "The 1942 Same-Sex Trials in Edmonton," 183–217.

31 "Murder Charge Reduced: Life Term in Prison Imposed in Stabbing," *Globe and Mail*, 24 Sept 1960, 4.

32 "George Klippert," District Court of Alberta (Calgary) series, Criminal files GR0023.007SF.0005.0002, Reel 3, 21–27 Mar, 4 Apr 1960. Provincial Archives of Alberta.

33 "City Man Remanded on Indecency Counts," *Calgary Herald*, 23 Mar 1960.

34 "George Klippert," District Court of Alberta (Calgary) series, Criminal files GR0023.007SF.0005.0002, Reel 3, 21–27 Mar, 4 Apr 1960. Provincial Archives of Alberta.

35 Gary Kinsman, "'Character Weaknesses' and 'Fruit Machines': Towards an Analysis of the Anti-Homosexual Security Campaign in the Canadian Civil Service," *Labour/Le travail* 35 (Spring 1995): 133–61.

36 Gary Kinsman, "The Canadian Cold War on Queers: Sexual Regulation and Resistance," in *Love, Hate, and Fear in Canada's Cold War*, ed. Richard Cavell (Toronto: University of Toronto Press, 2004), 109–32.

37 John Ibbitson, "Everett Klippert's Story: The Long, Late Redemption of a Man Punished for Being Gay in the 1960s," *Globe and Mail*, 27 Feb 2016, https://www.theglobeandmail.com/news/national/everett-klipperts-story/article28927305/.

38 Havelock Ellis, *Studies in The Psychology of Sex: Volume 2: Sexual Inversion* (Philadelphia: F. A. Davis, 1901), 1–65.

39 John Ibbitson, "Everett Klippert's Story," https://www.theglobeandmail.com/news/national/everett-klipperts-story/article28927305/.

40 Department of Justice Canada. Juvenile Delinquency in Canada: The Report of the Department of Justice Committee on Juvenile Delinquency, 1965, Queen's Printer, Ottawa: 1967, http://publications.gc.ca/collections/collection_2017/jus/JS22-1965-1-eng.pdf.

41 Marilyn Pilon, Canada's Legal Age of Consent to Sexual Activity. http://publications.gc.ca/Collection-R/LoPBdP/BP/prb993-e.htm.

42 Klippert v. The Queen, [1967] S.C.R. 822. Date: 1967-11-07. https://scc-csc.lexum.com/scc-csc/scc-csc/en/item/4738/index.do. There are no court cases or available arrest records for these four men.

43 1960 Canadian Criminal Code, S.C. 1953-54, c. 51. Part IV Sexual Offences, Public Morals and Disorderly Conduct. http://www.constancebackhouse.ca/fileadmin/website/1960.htm.

44 Klippert v. The Queen, [1967] S.C.R. 822. Date: 1967-11-07. https://scc-csc.lexum.com/scc-csc/scc-csc/en/item/4738/index.do

45 John Ibbitson, "Everett Klippert's story: The Long, Late Redemption of a Man Punished for Being Gay in the 1960s," *Globe and Mail*, 27 Feb 2016, https://www.theglobeandmail.com/news/national/everett-klipperts-story/article28927305/.

46 "Supreme Court Decision Means Homosexuals Can Face Imprisonment for Life," *Globe and Mail*, 8 Nov 1967.

47 "'Gross Indecency' Vague: Sex Law Revisions to Make Little Change in Practice, Study Says," *Globe and Mail*, 14 Jan 1969, 31.

48 Patricia Dawn Robertson, "William Wuttunee (1928–2015)," *Globe and Mail*, 4 Dec 2015.

49 Penney Kome, "Everett Klippert Was Represented by Western Canada's First Indigenous Lawyer," *rabble.ca Blogs*, 1 Dec 2017, http://www.rabble.ca/blogs/bloggers/other-hand/2017/12/everett-klippert-was-represented-western-canadas-first-indigenous.

50 Lewis Seal, "Trudeau Says Ouimet Committee May Study Homosexual Problem," *Globe and Mail*, 9 Nov 1967.

51 Cabinet Conclusion 3, Legislative Programme: Homosexual Law Reform, 27 Oct 1966, National Archives, http://www.nationalarchives.gov.uk/cabinetpapers/themes/homosexuality.htm#Sexual%20Offences%20Act%201967.

52 "Homosexuals Not Encouraged, Turner Says," *Globe and Mail*, 18 Apr 1969, 4.

53 Ibid.

54 1970 Canadian Criminal Code, S.C. 1953-54, c. 51. Part IV Sexual Offences, Public Morals and Disorderly Conduct. http://www.constancebackhouse.ca/fileadmin/website/1970.htm

55 Farrell Crook, "14 Publishers Refused to Distribute Article: Senators Describe Deletion of *Weekend* Story on Homosexuals as Censorship," *Globe and Mail*, 4 Mar 1970, 4.

56 Geoff Ellwand, "Everett Klippert: Canadian Legal History's Troubling Hero," *Canadian Bar Association Alberta Branch*, 2017. https://www.cba-alberta.org/Publications-Resources/Resources/Law-Matters/Law-Matters-Summer-2017/Everett-Klippert-Canadian-Legal-History-s-Troublin.

57 "Klippert's Case Helped Change the Law but He Remains in 'Preventative Detention,'" *Montreal Gazette*, 20 Dec 1969.

58 Ibbitson, "Everett Klippert's Story."

59 Everett Klippert's diary, Aug 1969. Image uploaded at Calgary Gay History, https://calgarygayhistory.ca/2019/02/21/news-from-yyc-gay-history/.

Director's Notes

Jason Mehmel

I still remember the first time I experienced this story. I was in Loft 112, a local literary hub in Calgary. This was in February 2016, at a workshop produced by Jonathan Brower at Third Street Theatre, as Third Street helped Natalie develop the script. Loft 112 is situated in the East Village . . . one of Calgary's first neighbourhoods. From my seat I could see out the tall windows into the parking lot across the street. Beyond that, I could see the Calgary Transit c-train line.

I could see the Calgary of today outside, while its past was being explored inside the room. It was feeling, that moment of past and present colliding, that hooked me. We are still walking down streets that Klippert walked, catching busses that are on the routes he drove as a bus driver, and eating at restaurants that have barely changed since the sixties!

It was important that Natalie's play be seen, and I wanted to help make that happen. It was wrong that more people didn't know about Klippert. I wanted to extend the reach as far as I could. When I tell people about it even now, their eyebrows go up. "That happened here?" More people needed to know this story.

This was also a chance to work with Natalie once again, continuing a personal and professional friendship that has persisted over many years. We make each other better, as artists and as friends. Natalie is one of the smartest writers I know, applying that intelligence to writing about deeply human problems and complications. She is also one of the funniest people I know. When we spend time together, it's mostly spent laughing. You might sense that laughter in this play.

Later, when working to produce the play, I did my best to get the right people in that room—my role and responsibility as a director as a steward for both Natalie's play and Klippert's story—and I did my best to make sure everyone could do their best job possible.

Presenting real lives and history creates exciting challenges. When working on a play, we can often make up the situation surrounding the play according to whatever we think the story needs. Here, we had to look to historical facts, and adjust our story to fit (this process almost always makes things more interesting, not less!). We would be discussing a scene location in the play's present, only to realize that an important building or reference point hadn't been constructed in the preceding scenes that take place in the 60s. As we discovered and filled in this map of the time, we found it would create resonances that with the scenes and characters throughout the work.

I am cisgendered straight white male. I say this to acknowledge that in working on this play I am working with stories and experiences that are not my own. In my cultural role as a director, it is important to me that I use the demographic privileges I possess to facilitate the telling and sharing of the kinds of stories and experiences found in this play, to present such stories and experiences to local audiences, and to boost the artists who are making this work. It was important to me to facilitate the sharing of Klippert's story and Natalie's play, specifically.

I was honoured to explore cultures and communities outside of my experience, and for the opportunity to become an ally to those communities. I can support those groups, and work together with them to support the structural changes in society that are urgently needed. I don't always get it right, and I thank the people of these communities for their patience as I continue to learn how to be a better ally.

I am grateful that I've had the opportunity to take part in presenting Klippert's story. Thank you for reading it.

Original Cast, Direction, and Crew

The play *Legislating Love* was premiered by Sage Theatre at the West Village Theatre in Calgary, Alberta. Opening night was 22 March 2018.

Cast
Handsome: Mark Bellamy
Tonya: Jenn Forgie
Everett: Matt McKinney
Maxine: Kathy Zaborsky

Direction
Director: Jason Mehmel
Assistant Director: Jay Northcott

Crew
Stage Manager: Michael Howard
Set and Lights: Terry Gunvordahl
Costume Design: Jordan Wieben
Sound Design: Travis McKinnon
Fight Direction: Laryssa Yanchak

The original cast of *Legislating Love*, from left to right: Matt McKinney, Jenn Forgie, Kathy Zaborsky, Mark Bellamy. Photograph by Jason Mehmel.

Acknowledgements

Natalie Meisner

This play was commissioned by *Third Street Theatre* then researched and developed in cooperation with Kevin Allen and Tereasa Maillie of the Calgary Gay History Project with research dramaturgy by Jonathan Brower of *Third Street Theatre*. A table reading was supported by the Alberta Playwrights Network. Personal interviews with Mr. Klippert's relatives, and the opportunity to spend time with his personal diaries and letters, were most helpful (thank you Donald Klippert, Katherine Griebel, and Sarah Griebel). Selected scenes have been given staged reads at Loft 112 to solicit feedback from community members and elders. Warmest gratitude to every person who shared their (often hard-won) life story to enrich this play. Also to Pamela Halstead, Chapelle Jaffe, Yvette Nolan, and Nathalie Kermoal who read and gave input on the play. *Legislating Love* was inspired, in part, by the Mount Royal University Life Writing Project that pairs senior citizens with creative writing students to craft their life stories. The Faculty of Arts Endeavour Fund supported the development of the play prior to the world premiere at Sage Theatre in Calgary in March 2018 (direction by Jason Mehmel).

Natalie Meisner is an award-winning playwright, professor of English, and Director of Changemaking at Mount Royal University. She is the author of *Double Pregnant*, *My Mommy, My Mama My Brother & Me*, and *Baddie One Shoe*. Her play *Boom Baby* won both the Canadian National Playwriting Award and the Alberta Playwriting Award in 2019.

Kevin Allen is research lead of the Calgary Gay History Project, and the author of *Our Past Matters: Stories of Gay Calgary*.

Tereasa Maillie is a writer and researcher with the Calgary Gay History Project. She is also a producer, playwright, and poet.

Jason Mehmel is a writer, producer, and director living in Calgary, Alberta. He is the Artistic Director of the Sage Theatre, and directed the premier production of *Legislating Love.*

BRAVE & BRILLIANT SERIES

SERIES EDITOR:
Aritha van Herk, Professor, English, University of Calgary
ISSN 2371-7238 (Print) ISSN 2371-7246 (Online)

Brave & Brilliant encompasses fiction, poetry, and everything in between and beyond. Bold and lively, each with its own strong and unique voice, Brave & Brilliant books entertain and engage readers with fresh and energetic approaches to storytelling and verse, in print or through innovative digital publication.

.